Contents

FRESH SOUTHERN PEACH COBBLER

Servings: 4 | Prep: 20m | Cooks: 40m | Total: 1h

NUTRITION FACTS

Calories: 562 | Carbohydrates: 99.4g | Fat: 17.6g | Protein: 3.5g | Cholesterol: 46mg

INGREDIENTS

- 8 fresh peaches - peeled, pitted and sliced into thin wedges
- 1/4 cup white sugar
- 1/4 cup white sugar
- 1 teaspoon ground cinnamon
- 1/4 cup brown sugar
- 1/4 cup brown sugar
- 1/4 teaspoon ground cinnamon
- 1 teaspoon baking powder
- 1/8 teaspoon ground nutmeg
- 1/2 teaspoon salt
- 1 teaspoon fresh lemon juice
- 6 tablespoons unsalted butter, chilled and cut into small pieces
- 2 teaspoons cornstarch
- 1/4 cup boiling water
- 1 cup all-purpose flour
- 3 tablespoons white sugar

DIRECTIONS

1. Preheat oven to 425 degrees F (220 degrees C).
2. In a large bowl, combine peaches, 1/4 cup white sugar, 1/4 cup brown sugar, 1/4 teaspoon cinnamon, nutmeg, lemon juice, and cornstarch. Toss to coat evenly, and pour into a 2 quart baking dish. Bake in preheated oven for 10 minutes.
3. Meanwhile, in a large bowl, combine flour, 1/4 cup white sugar, 1/4 cup brown sugar, baking powder, and salt. Blend in butter with your fingertips, or a pastry blender, until mixture resembles coarse meal. Stir in water until just combined.
4. Remove peaches from oven, and drop spoonfuls of topping over them. Sprinkle entire cobbler with the sugar and cinnamon mixture. Bake until topping is golden, about 30 minutes.

SWEET DINNER ROLLS

Servings: 16 | Prep: 20m | Cooks: 20m | Total: 2h20m

NUTRITION FACTS

Calories: 192 | Carbohydrates: 27.1g | Fat: 7.5g | Protein: 3.9g | Cholesterol: 30mg

INGREDIENTS

- 1/2 cup warm water (110 degrees F/45 degrees C)
- 1 teaspoon salt
- 1/2 cup warm milk
- 3 3/4 cups all-purpose flour
- 1 egg
- 1 (.25 ounce) package active dry yeast
- 1/3 cup butter, softened
- 1/4 cup butter, softened
- 1/3 cup white sugar

DIRECTIONS

1. Place water, milk, egg, 1/3 cup butter, sugar, salt, flour and yeast in the pan of the bread machine in the order recommended by the manufacturer. Select Dough/Knead and First Rise Cycle; press Start.
2. When cycle finishes, turn dough out onto a lightly floured surface. Divide dough in half. Roll each half into a 12 inch circle, spread 1/4 cup softened butter over entire round. Cut each circle into 8 wedges. Roll wedges starting at wide end; roll gently but tightly. Place point side down on ungreased cookie sheet. Cover with clean kitchen towel and put in a warm place, let rise 1 hour. Meanwhile, preheat oven to 400 degrees F (200 degrees C).
3. Bake in preheated oven for 10 to 15 minutes, until golden.

SWEET POTATO PIE

Servings: 8 | Prep: 30m | Cooks: 1h50m | Total: 2h20m

NUTRITION FACTS

Calories: 389 | Carbohydrates: 47.8g | Fat: 20.6g | Protein: 4.5g | Cholesterol: 78mg

INGREDIENTS

- 1 (1 pound) sweet potato
- 1/2 teaspoon ground nutmeg
- 1/2 cup butter, softened
- 1/2 teaspoon ground cinnamon
- 1 cup white sugar
- 1 teaspoon vanilla extract
- 1/2 cup milk
- 1 (9 inch) unbaked pie crust
- 2 eggs

DIRECTIONS

1. Boil sweet potato whole in skin for 40 to 50 minutes, or until done. Run cold water over the sweet potato, and remove the skin.
2. Break apart sweet potato in a bowl. Add butter, and mix well with mixer. Stir in sugar, milk, eggs, nutmeg, cinnamon and vanilla. Beat on medium speed until mixture is smooth. Pour filling into an unbaked pie crust.
3. Bake at 350 degrees F (175 degrees C) for 55 to 60 minutes, or until knife inserted in center comes out clean. Pie will puff up like a souffle, and then will sink down as it cools.

COLLEEN'S SLOW COOKER JAMBALAYA
Servings: 12 | Prep: 20m | Cooks: 8h | Total: 8h20m

NUTRITION FACTS

Calories: 234 | Carbohydrates: 6.1g | Fat: 13.6g | Protein: 20.2g | Cholesterol: 99mg

INGREDIENTS

- 1 pound skinless, boneless chicken breast halves - cut into 1 inch cubes
- 2 teaspoons dried oregano
- 1 pound andouille sausage, sliced
- 2 teaspoons dried parsley
- 1 (28 ounce) can diced tomatoes with juice
- 2 teaspoons Cajun seasoning
- 1 large onion, chopped
- 1 teaspoon cayenne pepper
- 1 large green bell pepper, chopped
- 1/2 teaspoon dried thyme
- 1 cup chopped celery
- 1 pound frozen cooked shrimp without tails
- 1 cup chicken broth

DIRECTIONS

1. In a slow cooker, mix the chicken, sausage, tomatoes with juice, onion, green bell pepper, celery, and broth. Season with oregano, parsley, Cajun seasoning, cayenne pepper, and thyme.
2. Cover, and cook 7 to 8 hours on Low, or 3 to 4 hours on High. Stir in the shrimp during the last 30 minutes of cook time.

KICKIN' COLLARD GREENS
Servings: 6 | Prep: 10m | Cooks: 1h | Total: 1h10m

NUTRITION FACTS

Calories: 127 | Carbohydrates: 7.9g | Fat: 9.2g | Protein: 4.4g | Cholesterol: 12mg

INGREDIENTS

- 1 tablespoon olive oil
- 1 teaspoon pepper
- 3 slices bacon
- 3 cups chicken broth
- 1 large onion, chopped
- 1 pinch red pepper flakes
- 2 cloves garlic, minced
- 1 pound fresh collard greens, cut into 2-inch pieces
- 1 teaspoon salt

DIRECTIONS

1. Heat oil in a large pot over medium-high heat. Add bacon, and cook until crisp. Remove bacon from pan, crumble and return to the pan. Add onion, and cook until tender, about 5 minutes. Add garlic, and cook until just fragrant. Add collard greens, and fry until they start to wilt.
2. Pour in chicken broth, and season with salt, pepper, and red pepper flakes. Reduce heat to low, cover, and simmer for 45 minutes, or until greens are tender.

KEY WEST CHICKEN

Servings: 4 | Prep: 15m | Cooks: 15m | Total: 1h | Additional: 30m

NUTRITION FACTS

Calories: 184 | Carbohydrates: 5.6g | Fat: 6.2g | Protein: 25.3g | Cholesterol: 67mg

INGREDIENTS

- 3 tablespoons soy sauce
- 1 teaspoon lime juice
- 1 tablespoon honey
- 1 teaspoon chopped garlic
- 1 tablespoon vegetable oil
- 4 skinless, boneless chicken breast halves

DIRECTIONS

1. In a shallow container, blend soy sauce, honey, vegetable oil, lime juice, and garlic. Place chicken breast halves into the mixture, and turn to coat. Cover, and marinate in the refrigerator at least 30 minutes.
2. Preheat an outdoor grill for high heat.

3. Lightly oil the grill grate. Discard marinade, and grill chicken 6 to 8 minutes on each side, until juices run clear.

SMOOTH SWEET TEA

Servings: 8 | Prep: 5m | Cooks: 15m | Total: 3h20m

NUTRITION FACTS

Calories: 73 | Carbohydrates: 18.7g | Fat: 0g | Protein: 0g | Cholesterol: 0mg

INGREDIENTS

- 1 pinch baking soda
- 3/4 cup white sugar
- 2 cups boiling water
- 6 cups cool water
- 6 tea bags

DIRECTIONS

1. Sprinkle a pinch of baking soda into a 64-ounce, heat-proof, glass pitcher. Pour in boiling water, and add tea bags. Cover, and allow to steep for 15 minutes.
2. Remove tea bags, and discard; stir in sugar until dissolved. Pour in cool water, then refrigerate until cold.

SCOTT HIBB'S AMAZING WHISKY GRILLED BABY BACK RIBS

Servings: 6 | Prep: 20m | Cooks: 2h40m | Total: 3h

NUTRITION FACTS

Calories: 1029 | Carbohydrates: 52.8g | Fat: 68g | Protein: 50.2g | Cholesterol: 234mg

INGREDIENTS

- 2 (2 pound) slabs baby back pork ribs
- 2 tablespoons Worcestershire sauce
- coarsely ground black pepper
- 2 teaspoons salt
- 1 tablespoon ground red chile pepper
- 1/4 teaspoon coarsely ground black pepper
- 2 1/4 tablespoons vegetable oil
- 11/4 teaspoons liquid smoke flavoring

- 1/2 cup minced onion
- 2 teaspoons whiskey
- 1 1/2 cups water
- 2 teaspoons garlic powder
- 1/2 cup tomato paste
- 1/4 teaspoon paprika
- 1/2 cup white vinegar
- 1/2 teaspoon onion powder
- 1/2 cup brown sugar
- 1 tablespoon dark molasses
- 2 1/2 tablespoons honey
- 1/2 tablespoon ground red chile pepper

DIRECTIONS

1. Preheat oven to 300 degree F (150 degrees C).
2. Cut each full rack of ribs in half, so that you have 4 half racks. Sprinkle salt and pepper (more pepper than salt), and 1 tablespoon chile pepper over meat. Wrap each half rack in aluminum foil. Bake for 2 1/2 hours.
3. Meanwhile, heat oil in a medium saucepan over medium heat. Cook and stir the onions in oil for 5 minutes. Stir in water, tomato paste, vinegar, brown sugar, honey, and Worcestershire sauce. Season with 2 teaspoons salt, 1/4 teaspoon black pepper, liquid smoke, whiskey, garlic powder, paprika, onion powder, dark molasses, and 1/2 tablespoon ground chile pepper. Bring mixture to a boil, then reduce heat. Simmer for 1 1/4 hours, uncovered, or until sauce thickens. Remove from heat, and set sauce aside.
4. Preheat an outdoor grill for high heat.
5. Remove the ribs from the oven, and let stand 10 minutes. Remove the racks from the foil, and place on the grill. Grill the ribs for 3 to 4 minutes on each side. Brush sauce on the ribs while they're grilling, just before you serve them (adding it too early will burn it).

THE BEST CHICKEN FRIED STEAK

Servings: 4 | Prep: 20m | Cooks: 20m | Total: 40m

NUTRITION FACTS

Calories: 791 | Carbohydrates: 71.1g | Fat: 34.3g | Protein: 47g | Cholesterol: 124mg

INGREDIENTS

- 4 (1/2 pound) beef cube steaks
- 1 egg
- 2 cups all-purpose flour
- 1 tablespoon hot pepper sauce (e.g. Tabasco)

- 2 teaspoons baking powder
- 2 cloves garlic, minced
- 1 teaspoon baking soda
- 3 cups vegetable shortening for deep frying
- 1 teaspoon black pepper
- 1/4 cup all-purpose flour
- 3/4 teaspoon salt
- 4 cups milk
- 1 1/2 cups buttermilk
- kosher salt and ground black pepper to taste

DIRECTIONS

1. Pound the steaks to about 1/4-inch thickness. Place 2 cups of flour in a shallow bowl. Stir together the baking powder, baking soda, pepper, and salt in a separate shallow bowl; stir in the buttermilk, egg, Tabasco Sauce, and garlic. Dredge each steak first in the flour, then in the batter, and again in the flour. Pat the flour onto the surface of each steak so they are completely coated with dry flour.
2. Heat the shortening in a deep cast-iron skillet to 325 degrees F (165 degrees C). Fry the steaks until evenly golden brown, 3 to 5 minutes per side. Place fried steaks on a plate with paper towels to drain. Drain the fat from the skillet, reserving 1/4 cup of the liquid and as much of the solid remnants as possible.
3. Return the skillet to medium-low heat with the reserved oil. Whisk the remaining flour into the oil. Scrape the bottom of the pan with a spatula to release solids into the gravy. Stir in the milk, raise the heat to medium, and bring the gravy to a simmer, cook until thick, 6 to 7 minutes. Season with kosher salt and pepper. Spoon the gravy over the steaks to serve.

AUTHENTIC LOUISIANA RED BEANS AND RICE

Servings: 8 | Prep: 25m | Cooks: 3h5m | Total: 11h30m | Additional: 8h

NUTRITION FACTS

Calories: 630 | Carbohydrates: 79.1g | Fat: 24.2g | Protein: 24g | Cholesterol: 33mg

INGREDIENTS

- 1 pound dry kidney beans
- 1/2 teaspoon cayenne pepper
- 1/4 cup olive oil
- 1 teaspoon dried thyme
- 1 large onion, chopped
- 1/4 teaspoon dried sage
- 1 green bell pepper, chopped
- 1 tablespoon dried parsley
- 2 tablespoons minced garlic

- 1 teaspoon Cajun seasoning
- 2 stalks celery, chopped
- 1 pound andouille sausage, sliced
- 6 cups water
- 4 cups water
- 2 bay leaves
- 2 cups long grain white rice

DIRECTIONS

1. Rinse beans, and then soak in a large pot of water overnight.
2. In a skillet, heat oil over medium heat. Cook onion, bell pepper, garlic, and celery in olive oil for 3 to 4 minutes.
3. Rinse beans, and transfer to a large pot with 6 cups water. Stir cooked vegetables into beans. Season with bay leaves, cayenne pepper, thyme, sage, parsley, and Cajun seasoning. Bring to a boil, and then reduce heat to medium-low. Simmer for 2 1/2 hours.
4. Stir sausage into beans, and continue to simmer for 30 minutes.
5. Meanwhile, prepare the rice. In a saucepan, bring water and rice to a boil. Reduce heat, cover, and simmer for 20 minutes. Serve beans over steamed white rice.

GARLIC CHICKEN FRIED CHICKEN

Servings: 4 | Prep: 20m | Cooks: 15m | Total: 35m

NUTRITION FACTS

Calories: 391 | Carbohydrates: 37.3g | Fat: 11.4g | Protein: 32.8g | Cholesterol: 116mg

INGREDIENTS

- 2 teaspoons garlic powder, or to taste
- 1 cup all-purpose flour
- 1 teaspoon ground black pepper
- 1/2 cup milk
- 1 teaspoon salt
- 1 egg
- 1 teaspoon paprika
- 4 skinless, boneless chicken breast halves - pounded thin
- 1/2 cup seasoned bread crumbs
- 1 cup oil for frying, or as needed

DIRECTIONS

1. In a shallow dish, mix together the garlic powder, pepper, salt, paprika, bread crumbs and flour. In a separate dish, whisk together the milk and egg.

2. Heat the oil in an electric skillet set to 350 degrees F (175 degrees C). Dip the chicken into the egg and milk, then dredge in the dry ingredients until evenly coated.
3. Fry chicken in the hot oil for about 5 minutes per side, or until the chicken is cooked through and juices run clear. Remove from the oil with a slotted spatula, and serve.

CHEF JOHN'S BUTTERMILK BISCUITS

Servings: 12 | Prep: 20m | Cooks: 15m | Total: 35m

NUTRITION FACTS

Calories: 143 | Carbohydrates: 17g | Fat: 7.1g | Protein: 2.8g | Cholesterol: 19mg

INGREDIENTS

- 2 cups all-purpose flour
- 7 tablespoons unsalted butter, chilled in freezer and cut into thin slices
- 2 teaspoons baking powder
- 3/4 cup cold buttermilk
- 1 teaspoon salt
- 2 tablespoons buttermilk for brushing
- 1/4 teaspoon baking soda

DIRECTIONS

1. Preheat oven to 425 degrees F (220 degrees C).
2. Line a baking sheet with a silicone baking mat or parchment paper.
3. Whisk flour, baking powder, salt, and baking soda together in a large bowl.
4. Cut butter into flour mixture with a pastry blender until the mixture resembles coarse crumbs, about 5 minutes.
5. Make a well in the center of butter and flour mixture. Pour in 3/4 cup buttermilk; stir until just combined.
6. Turn dough onto a floured work surface, pat together into a rectangle.
7. Fold the rectangle in thirds. Turn dough a half turn, gather any crumbs, and flatten back into a rectangle. Repeat twice more, folding and pressing dough a total of three times.
8. Roll dough on a floured surface to about 1/2 inch thick.
9. Cut out 12 biscuits using a 2 1/2-inch round biscuit cutter.
10. Transfer biscuits to the prepared baking sheet. Press an indent into the top of each biscuit with your thumb.
11. Brush the tops of biscuits with 2 tablespoons buttermilk.
12. Bake in the preheated oven until browned, about 15 minutes.

KENTUCKY BUTTER CAKE

Servings: 12 | Prep: 30m | Cooks: 1h | Total: 2h | Additional: 30m

NUTRITION FACTS

Calories: 508 | Carbohydrates: 71.1g | Fat: 22.6g | Protein: 6.2g | Cholesterol: 117mg

INGREDIENTS

- 3 cups unbleached all-purpose flour
- 2 teaspoons vanilla extract
- 2 cups white sugar
- 4 eggs
- 1 teaspoon salt
- 3/4 cup white sugar
- 1 teaspoon baking powder
- 1/3 cup butter
- 1/2 teaspoon baking soda
- 3 tablespoons water
- 1 cup buttermilk
- 2 teaspoons vanilla extract
- 1 cup butter

DIRECTIONS

1. Preheat oven to 325 degrees F (165 degrees C). Grease and flour a 10 inch Bundt pan.
2. In a large bowl, mix the flour, 2 cups sugar, salt, baking powder and baking soda. Blend in buttermilk, 1 cup of butter, 2 teaspoons of vanilla and 4 eggs. Beat for 3 minutes at medium speed. Pour batter into prepared pan.
3. Bake in preheated oven for 60 minutes, or until a wooden toothpick inserted into center of cake comes out clean. Prick holes in the still warm cake. Slowly pour sauce over cake. Let cake cool before removing from pan.
4. To Make Butter Sauce: In a saucepan combine the remaining 3/4 cups sugar, 1/3 cup butter, 2 teaspoons vanilla, and the water. Cook over medium heat, until fully melted and combined, but do not boil.

BANANAS FOSTER

Servings: 4 | Prep: 5m | Cooks: 15m | Total: 20m

NUTRITION FACTS

Calories: 534 | Carbohydrates: 73.2g | Fat: 23.8g | Protein: 4.6g | Cholesterol: 60mg

INGREDIENTS

- 1/4 cup butter
- 1/2 teaspoon ground cinnamon
- 2/3 cup dark brown sugar
- 3 bananas, peeled and sliced lengthwise and crosswise

- 3 1/2 tablespoons rum
- 1/4 cup coarsely chopped walnuts
- 1 1/2 teaspoons vanilla extract
- 1 pint vanilla ice cream

DIRECTIONS

1. In a large, deep skillet over medium heat, melt butter. Stir in sugar, rum, vanilla and cinnamon. When mixture begins to bubble, place bananas and walnuts in pan. Cook until bananas are hot, 1 to 2 minutes. Serve at once over vanilla ice cream.

KENTUCKY BISCUITS

Servings: 12 | Prep: 15m | Cooks: 15m | Total: 30m

NUTRITION FACTS

Calories: 154 | Carbohydrates: 17.9g | Fat: 8g | Protein: 2.7g | Cholesterol: 21mg

INGREDIENTS

- 2 cups all-purpose flour
- 1 tablespoon white sugar
- 2 1/2 teaspoons baking powder
- 1/2 cup butter
- 1/2 teaspoon baking soda
- 3/4 cup buttermilk
- 1 dash salt

DIRECTIONS

1. Preheat oven to 400 degrees F (200 degrees C).
2. In a bowl, mix the flour, baking powder, baking soda, salt, and sugar. Cut in 1/2 cup butter until the mixture resembles coarse crumbs. Mix in the buttermilk. Turn out onto a lightly floured surface, and knead 2 minutes. Transfer to an ungreased baking sheet, roll into a 6x6 inch square, and cut into 12 even sections. Do not separate.
3. Bake 15 minutes in the preheated oven, until a knife inserted in the center of the square comes out clean. Separate into biscuits, and serve hot.

BLACKBERRY COBBLER

Servings: 8 | Prep: 20m | Cooks: 25m | Total: 45m

NUTRITION FACTS

Calories: 318 | Carbohydrates: 58.4g | Fat: 9.1g | Protein: 2.7g | Cholesterol: 23mg

INGREDIENTS

- 1 cup all-purpose flour
- 1/4 cup boiling water
- 1 1/2 cups white sugar, divided
- 2 tablespoons cornstarch
- 1 teaspoon baking powder
- 1/4 cup cold water
- 1/2 teaspoon salt
- 1 tablespoon lemon juice
- 6 tablespoons cold butter
- 4 cups fresh blackberries, rinsed and drained

DIRECTIONS

1. Preheat oven to 400 degrees F (200 degrees C). Line a baking sheet with aluminum foil.
2. In a large bowl, mix the flour, 1/2 cup sugar, baking powder, and salt. Cut in butter until the mixture resembles coarse crumbs. Stir in 1/4 cup boiling water just until mixture is evenly moist.
3. In a separate bowl, dissolve the cornstarch in cold water. Mix in remaining 1 cup sugar, lemon juice, and blackberries. Transfer to a cast iron skillet, and bring to a boil, stirring frequently. Drop dough into the skillet by spoonfuls. Place skillet on the foil lined baking sheet.
4. Bake 25 minutes in the preheated oven, until dough is golden brown.

BUBBA'S JAMBALAYA

Servings: 12 | Prep: 25m | Cooks: 40m | Total: 1h5m

NUTRITION FACTS

Calories: 349 | Carbohydrates: 32.3g | Fat: 13.8g | Protein: 22.7g | Cholesterol: 72mg

INGREDIENTS

- 6 slices bacon, cut into 1 inch pieces
- 2 (14.5 ounce) cans crushed tomatoes, with liquid
- 1 cup chopped celery
- 2 cups beef broth
- 1 green bell pepper, seeded and chopped
- 2 cups chicken broth
- 1 onion, chopped
- 1 teaspoon dried thyme
- 1/2 pound cubed cooked ham
- 2 teaspoons Cajun seasoning
- 1/2 pound cubed cooked chicken
- 2 cups uncooked white rice

- 1/2 pound cubed smoked sausage
- 1/2 pound salad shrimp

DIRECTIONS

1. Heat a large pot over medium-high heat. Add bacon, and cook until crisp. Remove bacon pieces with a slotted spoon, and set aside. Add celery, bell pepper, and onion to the bacon drippings, and cook until tender.
2. Add the ham, chicken and sausage to the pot, and pour in the tomatoes, beef broth and chicken broth. Season with thyme and Cajun seasoning. Bring to a boil, and add the rice. Bring to a boil, then turn the heat to low, cover, and simmer for about 20 minutes, until the rice is tender.
3. Stir in the shrimp and bacon just before serving, and heat through. If you use uncooked shrimp, let it cook for about 5 minutes before serving.

OLD CHARLESTON STYLE SHRIMP AND GRITS

Servings: 8 | Prep: 30m | Cooks: 45m | Total: 1h15m

NUTRITION FACTS

Calories: 618 | Carbohydrates: 16.2g | Fat: 43.7g | Protein: 38.6g | Cholesterol: 270mg

INGREDIENTS

- 1 cup coarsely ground grits
- 1 green bell pepper, chopped
- 3 cups water
- 1 red bell pepper, chopped
- 2 teaspoons salt
- 1 yellow bell pepper, chopped
- 2 cups half-and-half
- 1 cup chopped onion
- 2 pounds uncooked shrimp, peeled and deveined
- 1 teaspoon minced garlic
- salt to taste
- 1/4 cup butter
- 1 pinch cayenne pepper, or to taste
- 1/4 cup all-purpose flour
- 1 lemon, juiced
- 1 cup chicken broth
- 1 pound andouille sausage, cut into 1/4-inch slices
- 1 tablespoon Worcestershire sauce
- 5 slices bacon
- 1 cup shredded sharp Cheddar cheese

DIRECTIONS

1. Bring water, grits, and salt to a boil in a heavy saucepan with a lid. Stir in half-and-half and simmer until grits are thickened and tender, 15 to 20 minutes. Set aside and keep warm.
2. Sprinkle shrimp with salt and cayenne pepper; drizzle with lemon juice. Set aside in a bowl.
3. Place andouille sausage slices in a large skillet over medium heat; fry sausage until browned, 5 to 8 minutes. Remove skillet from heat.
4. Cook bacon in a large skillet over medium-high heat, turning occasionally, until evenly browned, about 10 minutes. Retain bacon drippings in skillet. Transfer bacon slices to paper towels, let cool, and crumble.
5. Cook and stir green, red, and yellow bell peppers, onion, and garlic in the bacon drippings until the onion is translucent, about 8 minutes.
6. Stir shrimp and cooked vegetables into the andouille sausage and mix to combine.
7. Melt butter in a saucepan over medium heat; stir in flour to make a smooth paste. Turn heat to low and cook, stirring constantly, until the mixture is medium brown in color, 8 to 10 minutes. Watch carefully, mixture burns easily.
8. Pour the butter-flour mixture into the skillet with andouille sausage, shrimp, and vegetables. Place the skillet over medium heat and pour in chicken broth, bacon and Worcestershire sauce, cooking and stirring until the sauce thickens and the shrimp become opaque and bright pink, about 8 minutes.
9. Just before serving, mix sharp Cheddar cheese into grits until melted and grits are creamy and light yellow. Serve shrimp mixture over cheese grits.

TANGY HONEY GLAZED HAM

Servings: 20 | Prep: 15m | Cooks: 2h45m | Total: 3h

NUTRITION FACTS

Calories: 511 | Carbohydrates: 19.4g | Fat: 30.1g | Protein: 38.8g | Cholesterol: 111mg

INGREDIENTS

- 1 (10 pound) fully-cooked, bone-in ham
- 1/3 large orange, juiced and zested
- 11/4 cups packed dark brown sugar
- 2 tablespoons Dijon mustard
- 1/3 cup pineapple juice
- 1/4 teaspoon ground cloves
- 1/3 cup honey

DIRECTIONS

1. Preheat oven to 325 degrees F (165 degrees C). Place ham in a roasting pan
2. In a small saucepan, combine brown sugar, pineapple juice, honey, orange juice, orange zest, Dijon mustard, and ground cloves. Bring to a boil, reduce heat, and simmer for 5 to 10 minutes. Set aside.
3. Bake ham in preheated oven uncovered for 2 hours. Remove ham from oven, and brush with glaze. Bake for an additional 30 to 45 minutes, brushing ham with glaze every 10 minutes.

BEST FRIED GREEN TOMATOES

Servings: 4 | Prep: 5m | Cooks: 15m | Total: 20m

NUTRITION FACTS

Calories: 510 | Carbohydrates: 56.3g | Fat: 27g | Protein: 12.6g | Cholesterol: 95mg

INGREDIENTS

- 4 large green tomatoes
- 1/2 cup bread crumbs
- 2 eggs
- 2 teaspoons coarse kosher salt
- 1/2 cup milk
- 1/4 teaspoon ground black pepper
- 1 cup all-purpose flour
- 1 quart vegetable oil for frying
- 1/2 cup cornmeal

DIRECTIONS

1. Slice tomatoes 1/2 inch thick. Discard the ends. Watch Now
2. Whisk eggs and milk together in a medium-size bowl. Scoop flour onto a plate. Mix cornmeal, bread crumbs and salt and pepper on another plate. Dip tomatoes into flour to coat. Then dip the tomatoes into milk and egg mixture. Dredge in breadcrumbs to completely coat. Watch Now
3. In a large skillet, pour vegetable oil (enough so that there is 1/2 inch of oil in the pan) and heat over a medium heat. Place tomatoes into the frying pan in batches of 4 or 5, depending on the size of your skillet. Do not crowd the tomatoes, they should not touch each other. When the tomatoes are browned, flip and fry them on the other side. Drain them on paper towels. Watch Now.

SOUTHERN CANDIED SWEET POTATOES

Servings: 12 | Prep: 20m | Cooks: 1h | Total: 1h20m

NUTRITION FACTS

Calories: 397 | Carbohydrates: 79.4g | Fat: 7.9g | Protein: 3.7g | Cholesterol: 20mg

INGREDIENTS

- 6 large sweet potatoes
- 1 teaspoon ground nutmeg
- 1/2 cup butter
- 1 tablespoon vanilla extract
- 2 cups white sugar
- salt to taste

- 1 teaspoon ground cinnamon

DIRECTIONS

1. Peel the sweet potatoes and cut them into slices.
2. Melt the butter in a heavy skillet and add the sliced sweet potatoes.
3. Mix the sugar, cinnamon, nutmeg and salt. Cover the sweet potatoes with sugar mixture and stir. Cover skillet, reduce heat to low and cook for about 1 hour or until potatoes are "candied". They should be tender but a little hard around the edges. Also the sauce will turn dark. You will need to stir occasionally during the cooking. Stir in the vanilla just before serving. Serve hot.

SOUTHERN PIMENTO CHEESE

Servings: 12 | Prep: 10m | Cooks: 0m | Total: 10m

NUTRITION FACTS

Calories: 208 | Carbohydrates: 2.1g | Fat: 19.9g | Protein: 6.3g | Cholesterol: 44mg

INGREDIENTS

- 2 cups shredded extra-sharp Cheddar cheese
- 1/4 teaspoon onion powder
- 8 ounces cream cheese, softened
- 1 jalapeno pepper, seeded and minced (optional)
- 1/2 cup mayonnaise
- 1 (4 ounce) jar diced pimento, drained
- 1/4 teaspoon garlic powder
- salt and black pepper to taste
- 1/4 teaspoon ground cayenne pepper (optional)

DIRECTIONS

1. Place the Cheddar cheese, cream cheese, mayonnaise, garlic powder, cayenne pepper, onion powder, minced jalapeno, and pimento into the large bowl of a mixer. Beat at medium speed, with paddle if possible, until thoroughly combined. Season to taste with salt and black pepper.

BOUDREAUX'S ZYDECO STOMP GUMBO

Servings: 10 | Prep: 1h | Cooks: 1h | Total: 2h

NUTRITION FACTS

Calories: 437 | Carbohydrates: 18.5g | Fat: 29.3g | Protein: 21.7g | Cholesterol: 105mg

INGREDIENTS

- 1 tablespoon olive oil
- 6 stalks celery, diced
- 1 cup skinless, boneless chicken breast halves - chopped
- 4 roma (plum) tomatoes, diced
- 1/2 pound pork sausage links, thinly sliced
- 1 sweet onion, sliced
- 1 cup olive oil
- 1 (10 ounce) can diced tomatoes with green chile peppers, with liquid
- 1 cup all-purpose flour
- 2 tablespoons chopped fresh red chile peppers
- 2 tablespoons minced garlic
- 1 bunch fresh parsley, chopped
- 3 quarts chicken broth
- 1/4 cup Cajun seasoning
- 1 (12 fluid ounce) can or bottle beer
- 1 pound shrimp, peeled and deveined

DIRECTIONS

1. Heat oil in a medium skillet over medium high heat, and cook chicken until no longer pink and juices run clear. Stir in sausage, and cook until evenly browned. Drain chicken and sausage, and set aside.
2. In a large, heavy saucepan over medium heat, blend olive oil and flour to create a roux. Stir constantly until browned and bubbly. Mix in garlic, and cook about 1 minute.
3. Gradually stir chicken broth and beer into the roux mixture. Bring to a boil, and mix in celery, tomatoes, sweet onion, diced tomatoes with green chile peppers, red chile peppers, parsley, and Cajun seasoning. Reduce heat, cover, and simmer about 40 minutes, stirring often.
4. Mix chicken, sausage, and shrimp into the broth mixture. Cook, stirring frequently, about 20 minutes.

CINDY'S JAMBALAYA

Servings: 8 | Prep: 20m | Cooks: 45m | Total: 1h10m | Additional: 5m

NUTRITION FACTS

Calories: 284 | Carbohydrates: 24.6g | Fat: 11.5g | Protein: 18.4g | Cholesterol: 107mg

INGREDIENTS

- 1 tablespoon olive oil
- 1 cup uncooked white rice
- 1/2 pound smoked sausage (such as Conecuh(C)), cut into 1/4-inch thick slices
- 1 (14.5 ounce) can diced tomatoes with juice

- 1 large onion, chopped
- 1 tablespoon minced garlic
- 1 cup chopped green bell pepper
- 2 cups chicken broth
- 1 cup chopped celery
- 3 bay leaves
- salt to taste
- 1/4 teaspoon dried thyme leaves
- 1/2 teaspoon Cajun seasoning, or to taste
- 1 pound peeled and deveined medium shrimp (30-40 per pound)

DIRECTIONS

1. Heat the olive oil in a Dutch oven or large pot over medium heat. Stir in the sausage, and cook for 2 minutes. Add the onion, bell pepper, and celery; season with salt and Cajun seasoning. Cook and stir until the vegetables are soft, 6 to 8 minutes. Stir in the rice until evenly coated in the vegetable mixture, then pour in the tomatoes with juice, garlic, chicken broth, bay leaves, and thyme leaves. Bring to a simmer over medium-high heat, then reduce heat to medium-low, cover, and simmer 20 minutes.
2. After 20 minutes, stir in the shrimp, and cook 10 minutes uncovered until the shrimp turn pink and are no longer translucent in the center. Remove the pot from the heat, and let stand 5 minutes. Discard the bay leaves before serving.

TEXAS SHEET CAKE

Servings: 32 | Prep: 10m | Cooks: 20m | Total: 30m

NUTRITION FACTS

Calories: 256 | Carbohydrates: 35.8g | Fat: 12.5g | Protein: 2.4g | Cholesterol: 36mg

INGREDIENTS

- 2 cups all-purpose flour
- 5 tablespoons unsweetened cocoa powder
- 2 cups white sugar
- 6 tablespoons milk
- 1 teaspoon baking soda
- 5 tablespoons unsweetened cocoa powder
- 1/2 teaspoon salt
- 1/2 cup butter
- 1/2 cup sour cream
- 4 cups confectioners' sugar
- 2 eggs

- 1 teaspoon vanilla extract
- 1 cup butter
- 1 cup chopped walnuts (optional)
- 1 cup water

DIRECTIONS

1. Preheat oven to 350 degrees F (175 degrees C). Grease and flour a 10x15 inch pan.
2. Combine the flour, sugar, baking soda and salt. Beat in the sour cream and eggs. Set aside. Melt the butter on low in a saucepan, add the water and 5 tablespoons cocoa. Bring mixture to a boil then remove from heat. Allow to cool slightly, then stir cocoa mixture into the egg mixture, mixing until blended.
3. Pour batter into prepared pan. Bake in the preheated oven for 20 minutes, or until a toothpick inserted into the center comes out clean.
4. For the icing: In a large saucepan, combine the milk, 5 tablespoons cocoa and 1/2 cup butter. Bring to a boil, then remove from heat. Stir in the confectioners' sugar and vanilla, then fold in the nuts, mixing until blended. Spread frosting over warm cake.

EASY CAJUN JAMBALAYA

Servings: 6 | Prep: 15m | Cooks: 30m | Total: 45m

NUTRITION FACTS

Calories: 488 | Carbohydrates: 58.5g | Fat: 13.8g | Protein: 29.1g | Cholesterol: 74mg

INGREDIENTS

- 2 teaspoons olive oil
- 1/2 teaspoon onion powder
- 2 boneless skinless chicken breasts, cut into bite-size pieces
- salt and ground black pepper to taste
- 8 ounces kielbasa, diced
- 2 cups uncooked white rice
- 1 onion, diced
- 4 cups chicken stock
- 1 green bell pepper, diced
- 3 bay leaves
- 1/2 cup diced celery
- 2 teaspoons Worcestershire sauce
- 2 tablespoons chopped garlic
- 1 teaspoon hot pepper sauce
- 1/4 teaspoon cayenne pepper

DIRECTIONS

1. Heat oil in a large pot over medium high heat. Saute chicken and kielbasa until lightly browned, about 5 minutes. Stir in onion, bell pepper, celery and garlic. Season with cayenne, onion powder, salt and pepper. Cook 5 minutes, or until onion is tender and translucent. Add rice, then stir in chicken stock and bay leaves. Bring to a boil, then reduce heat, cover, and simmer 20 minutes, or until rice is tender. Stir in the Worcestershire sauce and hot pepper sauce.

PECAN PIE

Servings: 8 | Prep: 10m | Cooks: 1h | Total: 1h10m

NUTRITION FACTS

Calories: 512 | Carbohydrates: 65.1g | Fat: 27.3g | Protein: 5.4g | Cholesterol: 85mg

INGREDIENTS

- 1 3/4 cups white sugar
- 3 eggs
- 1/4 cup dark corn syrup
- 1/4 teaspoon salt
- 1/4 cup butter
- 1 teaspoon vanilla extract
- 1 tablespoon cold water
- 1 1/4 cups chopped pecans
- 2 teaspoons cornstarch
- 1 (9 inch) unbaked pie shell

DIRECTIONS

1. Preheat oven to 350 degrees F (175 degrees C).
2. In a medium saucepan, combine the sugar, corn syrup, butter, water, and cornstarch. Bring to a full boil, and remove from heat
3. In a large bowl, beat eggs until frothy. Gradually beat in cooked syrup mixture. Stir in salt, vanilla, and pecans. Pour into pie shell.
4. Bake in preheated oven for 45 to 50 minutes, or until filling is set

SLOW COOKER CREAMED CORN

Servings: 12 | Prep: 10m | Cooks: 4h | Total: 4h10m

NUTRITION FACTS

Calories: 192 | Carbohydrates: 13.7g | Fat: 15g | Protein: 3.4g | Cholesterol: 42mg

INGREDIENTS

- 1 1/4 (16 ounce) packages frozen corn kernels
- 1/2 cup milk
- 1 (8 ounce) package cream cheese
- 1 tablespoon white sugar
- 1/2 cup butter
- salt and pepper to taste

DIRECTIONS

1. In a slow cooker, combine corn, cream cheese, butter, milk, and sugar. Season with salt and pepper to taste.
2. Cook on High for 2 to 4 hours, or on Low for 4 to 6 hours.

IRRESISTIBLE PECAN PIE

Servings: 12 | Prep: 25m | Cooks: 1h | Total: 1h55m | Additional: 30m

NUTRITION FACTS

Calories: 452 | Carbohydrates: 49.1g | Fat: 28.2g | Protein: 5.4g | Cholesterol: 74mg

INGREDIENTS

- 1 1/2 cups all-purpose flour
- 2 tablespoons dark corn syrup
- 1/2 teaspoon salt
- 3/4 cup light brown sugar
- 2 tablespoons white sugar
- 3 tablespoons butter, melted
- 1/2 cup butter, chilled
- 1 pinch salt
- 4 tablespoons ice water
- 1/2 cup pecans, finely crushed
- 3 eggs, beaten
- 1 cup pecans, quartered
- 3/4 cup light corn syrup
- 1 cup pecan halves

DIRECTIONS

1. Preheat oven to 350 degrees F (175 degrees C).

2. To Make Crust: In a medium bowl, combine flour, salt and white sugar. Cut butter into flour mixture until it resembles coarse crumbs. Gradually sprinkle the water over the dry mixture, stirring until dough comes together enough to form a ball.

3. On a floured surface flatten dough ball with rolling pin. Roll out into a circle that is one inch larger than pie dish. Place pie shell into dish and refrigerate until pie filling is complete.

4. To Make Pie Filling: In a medium bowl, mix together eggs, light and dark corn syrups, brown sugar, butter, salt and finely crushed pecans. Spread quartered pecans over bottom of refrigerated pie crust. Pour syrup mixture over top of pecans, then arrange pecan halves on top of pie.

5. Bake in a preheated 350 degrees F (175 degrees C) oven for one hour or until firm; let cool for one hour before serving.

SOUTHERN FRIED CABBAGE

Servings: 6 | Prep: 5m | Cooks: 10m | Total: 15m

NUTRITION FACTS

Calories: 189 | Carbohydrates: 13.6g | Fat: 14.2g | Protein: 4.4g | Cholesterol: 5mg

INGREDIENTS

- 3 slices bacon, cut into thirds
- 1 teaspoon salt, or to taste
- 1/3 cup vegetable oil
- 1 teaspoon ground black pepper, or to taste
- 1 head cabbage, cored and sliced
- 1 white onion, chopped
- 1 pinch white sugar

DIRECTIONS

1. Place the bacon and vegetable oil into a large pot over medium heat. Season with salt and pepper. Cook for about 5 minutes, or until bacon is crisp. Add cabbage, onion, and sugar to the pot; cook and stir continuously for 5 minutes, until tender.

VICKI'S HUSH PUPPIES

Servings: 8 | Prep: 10m | Cooks: 30m | Total: 40m

NUTRITION FACTS

Calories: 277 | Carbohydrates: 36.7g | Fat: 12.9g | Protein: 4.6g | Cholesterol: 46mg

INGREDIENTS

- 2 eggs, beaten

- 1/2 cup white sugar
- 1 large onion, diced
- 1 cup self-rising flour
- 1 cup self-rising cornmeal
- 1 quart oil for frying

DIRECTIONS

1. In a medium bowl, mix together eggs, sugar, and onion. Blend in flour and cornmeal.
2. Heat 2 inches of oil to 365 degrees F (185 degrees C). Drop batter by rounded teaspoonfuls in hot oil, and fry until golden brown. Cook in small batches to maintain oil temperature. Drain briefly on paper towels. Serve hot.

SLOW COOKER CAROLINA BBQ

Servings: 10 | Prep: 15m | Cooks: 12m | Total: 12h15m

NUTRITION FACTS

Calories: 293 | Carbohydrates: 3.6g | Fat: 17.3g | Protein: 27.6g | Cholesterol: 90mg

INGREDIENTS

- 1 (5 pound) bone-in pork shoulder roast
- 2 tablespoons brown sugar
- 1 tablespoon salt
- 1 1/2 tablespoons hot pepper sauce
- ground black pepper
- 2 teaspoons cayenne pepper
- 1 1/2 cups apple cider vinegar
- 2 teaspoons crushed red pepper flakes

DIRECTIONS

1. Place the pork shoulder into a slow cooker and season with salt and pepper. Pour the vinegar around the pork. Cover, and cook on Low for 12 hours. Pork should easily pull apart into strands.
2. Remove the pork from the slow cooker and discard any bones. Strain out the liquid, and save 2 cups. Discard any extra. Shred the pork using tongs or two forks, and return to the slow cooker. Stir the brown sugar, hot pepper sauce, cayenne pepper, and red pepper flakes into the reserved sauce. Mix into the pork in the slow cooker. Cover and keep on Low setting until serving.

CAJUN CRAWFISH AND SHRIMP ETOUFFE

Servings: 6 | Prep: 20m | Cooks: 50m | Total: 1h10m

NUTRITION FACTS

Calories: 264 | Carbohydrates: 9g | Fat: 14g | Protein: 24.9g | Cholesterol: 196mg

INGREDIENTS

- 1/3 cup vegetable oil
- 1 small green bell pepper, diced
- 1/4 cup all-purpose flour
- 1 medium onion, chopped
- 2 cloves garlic, minced
- 2 stalks celery, diced
- 2 fresh tomatoes, chopped
- 2 tablespoons Louisiana-style hot sauce
- 1/3 teaspoon ground cayenne pepper (optional)
- 2 tablespoons seafood seasoning
- 1/2 teaspoon ground black pepper
- 1 cup fish stock
- 1 pound crawfish tails
- 1 pound medium shrimp - peeled and deveined

DIRECTIONS

1. Heat the oil in a heavy skillet over medium heat. Gradually stir in flour, and stir constantly until the mixture turns 'peanut butter' brown or darker, at least 15 or 20 minutes. I use a large fork with the flat side to the bottom of the pan in a side to side motion. This is your base sauce or 'Roux'. It is very important to stir this constantly. If by chance the roux burns, discard and start over.
2. Once the roux is browned, add the onions, garlic, celery and bell pepper to the skillet, and saute for about 5 minutes to soften. Stir in the chopped tomatoes and fish stock, and season with the seafood seasoning. Reduce heat to low, and simmer for about 20 minutes, stirring occasionally.
3. Season the sauce with hot pepper sauce and cayenne pepper (if using), and add the crawfish and shrimp. Cook for about 10 minutes, or until the shrimp are opaque.

FROGMORE STEW

Servings: 12 | Prep: 10m | Cooks: 30m | Total: 40m

NUTRITION FACTS

Calories: 499 | Carbohydrates: 39.1g | Fat: 15.5g | Protein: 52.6g | Cholesterol: 299mg

INGREDIENTS

- 6 quarts water
- 3/4 cup Old Bay Seasoning TM
- 2 pounds new red potatoes
- 2 pounds hot smoked sausage links, cut into 2 inch pieces
- 12 ears corn - husked, cleaned and quartered
- 4 pounds large fresh shrimp, unpeeled

DIRECTIONS

1. Bring water and Old Bay Seasoning to boil in a large stockpot.
2. Add potatoes and cook for 15 minutes. Add sausage and cook for 5 minutes more. Add corn and cook for another 5 minutes. Stir in the shrimp and cook until shrimp are pink, about 5 minutes. Drain immediately and serve.

GA PEACH POUND CAKE

Servings: 16 | Prep: 20m | Cooks: 1h10m | Total: 1h30m

NUTRITION FACTS

Calories: 307 | Carbohydrates: 44.1g | Fat: 13g | Protein: 4.1g | Cholesterol: 77mg

INGREDIENTS

- 1 cup butter or margarine, softened
- 3 cups all-purpose flour
- 2 cups white sugar
- 1 teaspoon baking powder
- 4 eggs
- 1/2 teaspoon salt
- 1 teaspoon vanilla extract
- 2 cups fresh peaches, pitted and choppe

DIRECTIONS

1. Preheat oven to 325 degrees F (165 degrees C). Butter a 10 inch tube pan and coat with white sugar.
2. In a large bowl, cream together the butter and sugar until light and fluffy. Add the eggs one at a time, beating well with each addition, then stir in the vanilla. Reserve 1/4 cup of flour for later, and sift together the remaining flour, baking powder and salt. Gradually stir into the creamed mixture. Use the reserved flour to coat the chopped peaches, then fold the floured peaches into the batter. Spread evenly into the prepared pan.

3. Bake for 60 to 70 minutes in the preheated oven, or until a toothpick inserted into the cake comes out clean. Allow cake to cool in the pan for 10 minutes, before inverting onto a wire rack to cool completely.

CAJUN CHICKEN AND SAUSAGE GUMBO
Servings: 10 | Prep: 45m | Cooks: 2h30m | Total: 3h15m

NUTRITION FACTS

Calories: 480 | Carbohydrates: 14.5g | Fat: 39.5g | Protein: 16.1g | Cholesterol: 56mg

INGREDIENTS

- 1 cup vegetable oil
- 4 cloves garlic, minced
- 1 cup all-purpose flour
- salt and pepper to taste
- 1 large onion, chopped
- Creole seasoning to taste
- 1 large green bell pepper, chopped
- 6 cups chicken broth
- 2 celery stalks, chopped
- 1 bay leaf
- 1 pound andouille or smoked sausage, sliced 1/4 inch thick
- 1 rotisserie chicken, boned and shredded

DIRECTIONS

1. Heat the oil in a Dutch oven over medium heat. When hot, whisk in flour. Continue whisking until the roux has cooked to the color of chocolate milk, 8 to 10 minutes. Be careful not to burn the roux. If you see black specks in the mixture, start over.
2. Stir onion, bell pepper, celery, and sausage into the roux; cook 5 minutes. Stir in the garlic and cook another 5 minutes. Season with salt, pepper, and Creole seasoning; blend thoroughly. Pour in the chicken broth and add the bay leaf. Bring to a boil over high heat, then reduce heat to medium-low, and simmer, uncovered, for 1 hour, stirring occasionally. Stir in the chicken, and simmer 1 hour more. Skim off any foam that floats to the top during the last hour.

SIMPLE COUNTRY RIBS
Servings: 4 | Prep: 10m | Cooks: 1h | Total: 1h10m

NUTRITION FACTS

Calories: 882 | Carbohydrates: 94.1g | Fat: 38.3g | Protein: 36.4g | Cholesterol: 150mg

INGREDIENTS

- 2 1/2 pounds pork spareribs
- 1 teaspoon salt
- 2 (18 ounce) bottles barbeque sauce
- 1/2 teaspoon ground black pepper
- 1 onion, quartered

DIRECTIONS

1. Place spareribs in a large stock pot with barbeque sauce, onion, salt, and pepper. Pour in enough water to cover. Bring to a low boil, and cook approximately 40 minutes
2. Preheat grill for high heat.
3. Lightly oil grate. Remove spareribs from the stock pot, and place on the prepared grill. Use the barbeque sauce in the saucepan to baste ribs while cooking. Grill ribs, basting and turning frequently, for 20 minutes, or until nicely browned.

MAYONNAISE BISCUITS

Servings: 12 | Prep: 10m | Cooks: 12m | Total: 22m

NUTRITION FACTS

Calories: 133 | Carbohydrates: 16.6g | Fat: 6.1g | Protein: 2.8g | Cholesterol: 4mg

INGREDIENTS

- 2 cups self-rising flour
- 1 cup milk
- 6 tablespoons mayonnaise

DIRECTIONS

1. Preheat oven to 400 degrees F (200 degrees C).
2. In a large bowl, stir together flour, milk, and mayonnaise until just blended. Drop by spoonfuls onto lightly greased baking sheets.
3. Bake for 12 minutes in the preheated oven, or until golden brown.

SOUTHERN PULLED PORK

Servings: 6 | Prep: 30m | Cooks: 6h | Total: 6h30m

NUTRITION FACTS

Calories: 178 | Carbohydrates: 2.9g | Fat: 10.1g | Protein: 17.9g | Cholesterol: 58mg

INGREDIENTS

- 1 tablespoon butter
- 4 cloves garlic, crushed
- 2 pounds boneless pork roast
- 4 cups water
- 1 tablespoon Cajun seasoning
- 1 tablespoon liquid smoke flavoring
- 1 medium onion, chopped

DIRECTIONS

1. Cut the pork roast into large chunks. Season generously with the Cajun seasoning. Melt butter in a large skillet over medium-high heat. Add pork, and brown on all sides. Remove from the skillet, and transfer to a slow cooker.
2. Add the onion and garlic to the skillet, and cook for a few minutes until tender. Stir in the water scraping the bottom to include all of the browned pork bits from the bottom of the pan, then pour the whole mixture into the slow cooker with the pork. Stir in liquid smoke flavoring.
3. Cover, and cook on High for 6 hours, or until meat is falling apart when pierced with a fork. Remove pieces of pork from the slow cooker, and shred. Return to the slow cooker to keep warm while serving.

EASY RED BEANS AND RICE

Servings: 8 | Prep: 10m | Cooks: 30m | Total: 40m

NUTRITION FACTS

Calories: 289 | Carbohydrates: 42.4g | Fat: 5.7g | Protein: 16.3g | Cholesterol: 35mg

INGREDIENTS

- 2 cups water
- 1 (16 ounce) package turkey kielbasa, cut diagonally into 1/4 inch slices
- 1 cup uncooked rice
- 1 green bell pepper, chopped
- 1 onion, chopped
- 1 clove chopped garlic
- 2 (15 ounce) cans canned kidney beans, drained
- 1 (16 ounce) can whole peeled tomatoes, chopped
- 1/2 teaspoon dried oregano
- salt to taste
- 1/2 teaspoon pepper

DIRECTIONS

1. In a saucepan, bring water to a boil. Add rice and stir. Reduce heat, cover and simmer for 20 minutes.
2. In a large skillet over low heat, cook sausage for 5 minutes. Stir in onion, green pepper and garlic; saute until tender. Pour in beans and tomatoes with juice. Season with oregano, salt and pepper. Simmer uncovered for 20 minutes. Serve over rice.

ROASTED OKRA

Servings: 3 | Prep: 5m | Cooks: 15m | Total: 20m

NUTRITION FACTS

Calories: 65 | Carbohydrates: 5.9g | Fat: 4.6g | Protein: 1.6g | Cholesterol: 0mg

INGREDIENTS

- 18 fresh okra pods, sliced 1/3 inch thick
- 1 tablespoon olive oil
- 2 teaspoons kosher salt, or to taste
- 2 teaspoons black pepper, or to taste

DIRECTIONS

1. Preheat an oven to 425 degrees F (220 degrees C).
2. Arrange the okra slices in one layer on a foil lined cookie sheet. Drizzle with olive oil and sprinkle with salt and pepper. Bake in the preheated oven for 10 to 15 minutes.

PEACH COBBLER

Servings: 8 | Prep: 15m | Cooks: 30m | Total: 45m

NUTRITION FACTS

Calories: 299 | Carbohydrates: 46.8g | Fat: 11.9g | Protein: 3.2g | Cholesterol: 2mg

INGREDIENTS

- 1 cup all-purpose flour
- 1/2 cup white sugar
- 1/2 cup brown suga
- 2 teaspoons baking powder
- 1/2 teaspoon salt

- 1 teaspoon vanilla extract
- 3/4 cup milk
- 1/2 cup margarine, melted
- 1 (29 ounce) can sliced canned peaches, drained
- 1 teaspoon ground cinnamon

DIRECTIONS

1. Preheat oven to 400 degrees F (200 degrees C). Grease a 9x9-inch baking dish.
2. In a large bowl, combine flour, brown sugar, white sugar, baking powder, salt, and vanilla. Pour milk into dry ingredients, and then stir in melted margarine. Mix thoroughly.
3. Pour mixture into prepared baking pan. Arrange peaches on top and sprinkle with cinnamon. Bake in preheated oven until golden brown, about 30 minutes.

DAVE'S LOW COUNTRY BOIL

Servings: 15 | Prep: 30m | Cooks: 30m | Total: 1h

NUTRITION FACTS

Calories: 722 | Carbohydrates: 45.8g | Fat: 29.4g | Protein: 67.6g | Cholesterol: 333mg

INGREDIENTS

- 1 tablespoon seafood seasoning (such as Old Bay), or to taste
- 5 pounds new potatoes
- 8 ears fresh corn, husks and silks removed
- 3 (16 ounce) packages cooked kielbasa sausage, cut into 1 inch pieces
- 5 pounds whole crab, broken into pieces
- 4 pounds fresh shrimp, peeled and deveined

DIRECTIONS

1. Heat a large pot of water over an outdoor cooker, or medium-high heat indoors. Add Old Bay Seasoning to taste, and bring to a boil. Add potatoes, and sausage, and cook for about 10 minutes. Add the corn and crab; cook for another 5 minutes, then add the shrimp when everything else is almost done, and cook for another 3 or 4 minutes.
2. Drain off the water and pour the contents out onto a picnic table covered with newspaper. Grab a paper plate and a beer and enjoy.

BEST BREAD PUDDING WITH VANILLA SAUCE

Servings: 8 | Prep: 15m | Cooks: 1h | Total: 1h25m

NUTRITION FACTS

Calories: 546 | Carbohydrates: 91.7g | Fat: 16.5g | Protein: 10.5g | Cholesterol: 129mg

INGREDIENTS

- 3 eggs, beaten
- 1 1/2 cups white sugar
- 2 tablespoons light brown sugar
- 1/2 teaspoon ground cinnamon
- 1/4 cup butter, melted
- 3 cups whole milk
- 10 slices hearty farmhouse-style bread, toasted and cut into cubes
- 1 cup raisins
- 1/2 cup light brown sugar
- 1 tablespoon all-purpose flour
- 1 pinch ground cinnamon
- 1 egg
- 2 tablespoons butter, melted
- 1 1/4 cups whole milk
- 1 pinch salt
- 1 tablespoon vanilla extract

DIRECTIONS

1. Preheat oven to 375 degrees F (190 degrees C). Grease a 2-quart baking dish.
2. In a mixing bowl, whisk 3 eggs, white sugar, 2 tablespoons of light brown sugar, 1/2 teaspoon of cinnamon, 1/4 cup of butter, and 3 cups of whole milk together, and gently stir in the bread cubes and raisins. Lightly spoon the mixture into the prepared baking dish.
3. Bake in the preheated oven until browned and set in the middle, 50 to 55 minutes; cover the dish with foil after 30 minutes to prevent excessive browning. Let the pudding stand for 10 minutes before serving.
4. For vanilla sauce, whisk 1/2 cup of light brown sugar, the flour, a pinch of cinnamon, 1 egg, 2 tablespoons of melted butter, 1 1/4 cups of whole milk,and salt together in a heavy saucepan until smooth. Heat over medium heat, whisking constantly, until thickened and the sauce coats the back of a spoon, 10 to 12 minutes. Stir in the vanilla extract. Pour sauce over warm bread pudding, or serve on the side in a bowl.

BARLOW'S BLACKENED CATFISH
Servings: 4 | Prep: 10m | Cooks: 40m | Total: 50m

NUTRITION FACTS

Calories: 368 | Carbohydrates: 8.5g | Fat: 29.8g | Protein: 17.4g | Cholesterol: 72mg

INGREDIENTS

- 2 teaspoons cayenne pepper
- 2 teaspoons garlic powder
- 2 teaspoons lemon pepper
- 2 teaspoons salt
- 2 teaspoons pepper
- 1 pound catfish fillets
- 2 tablespoons butter
- 1 cup Italian-style salad dressing

DIRECTIONS

1. Preheat oven to 350 degrees F (175 degrees C). Lightly grease a medium baking dish.
2. In a shallow, medium bowl, mix cayenne pepper, lemon pepper, garlic powder, salt and pepper.
3. Brush both sides of catfish fillets with butter. Rub fillets with the cayenne pepper mixture on both sides.
4. Heat a large heavy skillet over medium-high heat until really hot. Add fillets, and fry approximately 2 minutes on each side, until slightly blackened.
5. Arrange blackened fillets in a single layer in the prepared baking dish, and coat with Italian-style salad dressing. Bake 30 to 35 minutes in the preheated oven, until fish is easily flaked with a fork.

RATATOUILLE BAKE

Servings: 6 | Prep: 15m | Cooks: 45m | Total: 1h

NUTRITION FACTS

Calories: 188 | Carbohydrates: 22g | Fat: 7.6g | Protein: 9.7g | Cholesterol: 24mg

INGREDIENTS

- 1 tablespoon olive oil
- 5 cloves garlic, minced
- 1 onion, chopped
- 2 cups peeled and diced eggplant
- 2 cups chopped zucchini
- 1 green bell pepper, chopped
- 1 (14.5 ounce) can diced tomatoes
- 1 tablespoon dried basil

- 1 tablespoon dried parsley
- 1/2 teaspoon salt
- 1/8 teaspoon black pepper
- 1 (8 ounce) package frozen cheese ravioli
- 3/4 cup shredded mozzarella cheese

DIRECTIONS

1. Preheat oven to 350 degrees F (175 degrees C); spray a 2 1/2-quart baking dish with cooking spray.
2. Heat the olive oil in a large skillet over medium heat; cook and stir the garlic, onion, and eggplant with the garlic until the vegetables have begun to soften, about 8 minutes. Stir in the zucchini, bell pepper, tomatoes, basil, parsley, salt, and black pepper; bring the mixture to a boil, stirring frequently. Reduce heat to medium-low and simmer until the vegetables are tender, about 20 minutes.
3. Cook the frozen ravioli as directed on the package; drain. Spread the cooked ravioli in a layer into the bottom of the prepared baking dish; spoon the hot vegetables over the ravioli. Sprinkle with the cheese.
4. Bake in the preheated oven until the casserole is bubbling and the cheese is melted, about 20 minutes.

GET A HUSBAND BRUNSWICK STEW

Servings: 16 | Prep: 30m | Cooks: 3h | Total: 3h30m

NUTRITION FACTS

Calories: 380 | Carbohydrates: 25.3g | Fat: 18.8g | Protein: 28.5g | Cholesterol: 90mg

INGREDIENTS

- 1 tablespoon olive oil
- 1 cup ketchup
- 1 cup chopped onions
- 1/2 cup hickory flavored barbeque sauce
- 2 stalks celery, chopped
- salt and pepper to taste
- 1 1/2 pounds ground pork
- hot sauce to taste (optional)
- 1 1/2 pounds ground beef
- 1 green bell pepper
- 1 (3 pound) whole cooked chicken, deboned and shredded
- 3 (14.75 ounce) cans cream style corn

- 3 (14.5 ounce) cans whole peeled tomatoes with liquid, chopped

DIRECTIONS

1. Heat the olive oil in a large skillet, and saute the onions and celery until soft. Mix in the pork and beef, and cook until evenly browned. Do not drain.
2. Transfer the pork and beef mixture to a large stock pot over low heat. Stir in the shredded chicken, tomatoes and their liquid, ketchup, and barbeque sauce. Season with salt, pepper, and hot sauce. Place the whole green pepper into the mixture. Cook, stirring occasionally, 2 hours, or until thickened.
3. Stir the cream style corn into the stew mixture. Continue cooking 1 hour, or to desired consistency. Remove the green pepper; chop and return to the stew or discard.

GRANDMA'S IRON SKILLET APPLE PIE

Servings: 8 | Prep: 15m | Cooks: 45m | Total: 1h15m | Additional:15m

NUTRITION FACTS

Calories: 734 | Carbohydrates: 107.8g | Fat: 33.7g | Protein: 3.4g | Cholesterol: 49mg

INGREDIENTS

- 1/2 cup butter
- 1 cup white sugar, divided
- 1 cup brown sugar
- 2 teaspoons ground cinnamon, divided
- 5 Granny Smith apples -- peeled, cored, quartered, and thinly sliced
- 1/4 cup white sugar
- 3 (9 inch) refrigerated prerolled pie crusts
- 1 tablespoon butter, cut into small chunk

DIRECTIONS

1. Preheat oven to 350 degrees F (175 degrees C).
2. Place 1/2 cup butter into a heavy cast iron skillet, and melt butter in the oven. Remove skillet and sprinkle with brown sugar; return to oven to heat while you prepare the apples.
3. Remove skillet, and place 1 refrigerated pie crust on top of the brown sugar. Top the pie crust with half the sliced apples. Sprinkle apples with 1/2 cup of sugar and 1 teaspoon of cinnamon; place a second pie crust over the apples; top the second crust with the remaining apples, and sprinkle with 1/2 cup sugar and 1 teaspoon cinnamon. Top with the third crust; sprinkle the top crust with 1/4 cup sugar, and dot with 1 tablespoon of butter. Cut 4 slits into the top crust for steam.
4. Bake in the preheated oven until the apples are tender and the crust is golden brown, about 45 minutes. Serve warm.

CHEF JOHN'S SHRIMP ETOUFFEE

Servings: 4 | Prep: 35m | Cooks: 20m | Total: 1h15m

NUTRITION FACTS

Calories: 424 | Carbohydrates: 30.2g | Fat: 14.7g | Protein: 40.8g | Cholesterol: 369mg

INGREDIENTS

- 3/4 teaspoon paprika
- 1/4 teaspoon ground thyme
- 1/4 teaspoon dried oregano
- 1/4 teaspoon cayenne pepper
- 1/4 teaspoon garlic powder
- 1/4 teaspoon onion powder
- 1/4 teaspoon white pepper
- 1/4 teaspoon ground black pepper
- 2 pounds shrimp, peeled and deveined
- 1/2 teaspoon salt
- 1 tablespoon vegetable oil
- 3 tablespoons butter
- 1/3 cup diced onion
- 1/3 cup diced green bell pepper
- 1/3 cup thinly sliced celery
- 2 tablespoons all-purpose flour, or as needed
- 1/2 cup diced tomatoes
- 1 3/4 cups chicken stock, or as needed
- 1/2 teaspoon Worcestershire sauce
- 1 dash hot sauce, or more to taste
- salt to taste
- 1/4 cup sliced green onions
- 2 cups cooked rice, or to taste

DIRECTIONS

1. Whisk paprika, thyme, oregano, cayenne pepper, garlic powder, onion powder, white pepper, and black pepper together in a small bowl.

2. Drain shrimp in a colander for at least 15 minutes. Transfer to a bowl lined with paper towels and dry shrimp for about 3 minutes. Remove paper towels from bowl and season shrimp with 1 teaspoon salt and 1 teaspoon spice blend. Toss to coat shrimp with spice blend.

3. Heat vegetable oil a large heavy skillet over high heat until oil is smoking hot. Cook shrimp in the hot oil without stirring for 1 minute; stir, and cook 1 minute more.

4. Transfer shrimp to a large bowl. Let stand until juice forms in bowl. Strain shrimp juices into chicken stock to total 2 cups, adding more chicken stock if necessary.

5. Melt butter in large skillet over medium heat until butter begins to turn tan at the edges. Saute onion, celery, and green pepper in hot butter until softened, about 5 minutes. Pour in remaining spice blend.

6. Sprinkle flour into vegetable mixture and saute until combined, 3 to 4 minutes. Stir in tomatoes; cook until tomato juices begin to brown on bottom of pan, about 3 minutes. Whisk stock into vegetable mixture, stirring until smooth. Bring to a simmer and cook until slightly thickened and reduced to a gravy consistency, 3 to 5 minutes. Stir in Worcestershire sauce and hot sauce. Season with salt to taste.

7. Stir shrimp into etouffee sauce; let simmer until shrimp are cooked all the way through and no longer translucent, about 1 minute.

8. Garnish with green onions and a dusting of cayenne pepper. Pour over rice in large, shallow bowls.

SAUSAGE GRAVY

Servings: 8 | Prep: 5m | Cooks: 25m | Total: 30m

NUTRITION FACTS

Calories: 344 | Carbohydrates: 7.9g | Fat: 29.9g | Protein: 10.1g | Cholesterol: 51mg

INGREDIENTS

- 1 pound ground pork sausage
- 3 cups milk
- 3 tablespoons bacon grease
- 1/2 teaspoon salt
- 1/4 cup all-purpose flour
- 1/4 teaspoon ground black peppe

DIRECTIONS

1. Brown sausage in a large skillet over medium-high heat. Set aside, leaving the drippings in the skillet.
2. Mix bacon grease into the sausage drippings. Reduce heat to medium, combine with flour, and stir constantly until mixture just turns golden brown.
3. Gradually whisk milk into skillet. When the mixture is smooth, thickened, and begins to bubble, return the sausage to skillet. Season with salt and pepper. Reduce heat, and simmer for about 15 minutes.

BEER AND BROWN SUGAR STEAK MARINADE

Servings: 4 | Prep: 30m | Cooks: 15m | Total: 1h10m

NUTRITION FACTS

Calories: 390 | Carbohydrates: 9.2g | Fat: 20.8g | Protein: 38.1g | Cholesterol: 121mg

INGREDIENTS

- 2 (16 ounce) beef sirloin steaks
- 1/4 cup dark beer
- 2 tablespoons teriyaki sauce
- 2 tablespoons brown sugar
- 1/2 teaspoon seasoned salt
- 1/2 teaspoon black pepper
- 1/2 teaspoon garlic powder

DIRECTIONS

1. Preheat grill for high heat.
2. Use a fork to poke holes all over the surface of the steaks, and place steaks in a large baking dish. In a bowl, mix together beer, teriyaki sauce, and brown sugar. Pour sauce over steaks, and let sit about 5 minutes. Sprinkle with 1/2 the seasoned salt, pepper, and garlic powder; set aside for 10 minutes. Turn steaks over, sprinkle with remaining seasoned salt, pepper, and garlic powder, and continue marinating for 10 more minutes.
3. Remove steaks from marinade. Pour marinade into a small saucepan, bring to a boil, and cook for several minutes.
4. Lightly oil the grill grate. Grill steaks for 7 minutes per side, or to desired doneness. During the last few minutes of grilling, baste steaks with boiled marinade to enhance the flavor and ensure juiciness.

COUNTRY-STYLE STEAK

Servings: 4 | Prep: 15m | Cooks: 2h20m | Total: 2h35m

NUTRITION FACTS

Calories: 355 | Carbohydrates: 24.6g | Fat: 19.9g | Protein: 18.3g | Cholesterol: 27mg

INGREDIENTS

- 1 cup all-purpose flour
- 1 teaspoon cracked black pepper
- 1 teaspoon seasoned salt
- 1/4 teaspoon garlic powder (optional)
- 1 pound beef cube steaks
- 1/2 cup olive oil
- 2 cups beef broth

DIRECTIONS

1. Preheat oven to 350 degrees F (175 degrees C).

2. Mix the flour, black pepper, seasoned salt, and garlic powder together in a shallow bowl, and coat the cube steaks thoroughly with the flour mixture, patting the flour onto the steaks to get a good coating. Retain 3 tablespoons of seasoned flour.

3. Heat the olive oil in a skillet over medium heat, and pan-fry the cube steaks until golden brown on both sides, about 5 minutes per side. Place the steaks into a 9x12-inch baking dish. Whisk the retained seasoned flour into the beef broth until smooth, and pour the broth over the steaks. Cover the dish with aluminum foil.

4. Bake in the preheated oven until the meat is tender and the gravy has thickened, about 2 hours.

OVEN BAKED JAMBALAYA

Servings: 16 | Prep: 45m | Cooks: 2h | Total: 2h45m

NUTRITION FACTS

Calories: 541 | Carbohydrates: 47.6g | Fat: 25.8g | Protein: 28.5g | Cholesterol: 125mg

INGREDIENTS

- 1/2 cup butter
- 4 teaspoons Worcestershire sauce
- 1 large onion, diced
- 2 (28 ounce) cans whole peeled tomatoes
- 1 large green bell pepper, chopped
- 7 cups chicken stock
- 4 stalks celery, chopped
- 3 cups chopped cooked ham
- 4 cloves garlic, minced
- 3 cups cooked andouille sausage, sliced
- 1 (6 ounce) can tomato paste
- 3 cups cooked chicken, cut into bite-sized pieces
- 3 bay leaves
- 3 cups frozen cooked shrimp
- 3 tablespoons Creole seasoning blend (such as the one linked in the footnote)
- 4 cups uncooked long-grain white rice

DIRECTIONS

1. Preheat oven to 350 degrees F (175 degrees C).

2. Melt butter in large stock pot. Saute onion, green pepper, celery and garlic until tender, being careful not to burn the garlic. Add tomato paste and cook to brown slightly, stirring constantly. Stir in bay leaves, Creole seasoning blend and Worcestershire sauce. Pour into a large roasting pan. Squeeze tomatoes to break up into pieces, and add to mixture in pan. Stir in juice from tomatoes, chicken stock, ham, sausage, chicken, shrimp and rice. Mix well. Cover tightly with aluminum foil.
3. Bake in preheated oven for 1 1/2 hours, stirring once halfway through baking time. Remove bay leaves before serving.

PEACH COBBLER
Servings: 6 | Prep: 20m | Cooks: 45m | Total: 1h10m

NUTRITION FACTS

Calories: 672 | Carbohydrates: 112.7g | Fat: 24g | Protein: 4.7g | Cholesterol: 19mg

INGREDIENTS

- resh peaches - peeled, pitted, and sliced
- 1 teaspoon ground cinnamon
- 1 1/2 cups white sugar
- 1/2 cup shortening
- 1 cup white sugar
- 1 1/2 cups all-purpose flour
- 2 teaspoons baking powder
- 1/2 teaspoon salt
- 1 cup milk
- 2 cups boiling water
- 3 tablespoons butter

DIRECTIONS

1. Combine rice and water in a medium saucepan. Bring to a boil over high heat. Reduce heat to low, cover with lid, and allow to steam until tender, about 20 minutes.
2. While rice is cooking, grind peanuts in a blender and set aside. Heat the margarine in a skillet over medium heat. Stir in the onion; cook and stir until the onion has softened and turned golden brown about 10 minutes. Stir in ginger, carrots, and salt to taste. Reduce heat to low and cover to steam 5 minutes. Stir in cayenne pepper and peanuts. When rice is done, add it to skillet and stir gently to combine with other ingredients. Garnish with chopped cilantro.

TEXAS RANCH POTATO SALAD
Servings: 16 | Prep: 30m | Cooks: 30m | Total: 1h

NUTRITION FACTS

Calories: 353 | Carbohydrates: 24.8g | Fat: 25.9g | Protein: 6.5g | Cholesterol: 21mg

INGREDIENTS

- 1 (1 ounce) package ranch dressing mix
- 2 cups mayonnaise
- 3/4 cup chopped green onion
- 1 pound bacon slices
- 5 pounds unpeeled red potatoes

DIRECTIONS

1. Bring a large pot of lightly salted water to a boil. Add whole potatoes, and cook until tender, 15 to 20 minutes. Drain, run under cold water to cool, and chop into 1 inch cubes. Transfer to a large serving bowl, and refrigerate until completely chilled, about 2 hours.

2. In a small bowl, stir together the ranch dressing mix, mayonnaise and green onion. Cover, and refrigerate for about 2 hours to blend flavors.

3. Wrap bacon in paper towels and place on a plate. Cook in the microwave until crisp, about 15 minutes depending on the power of your microwave. Cool.

4. Stir the mayonnaise mixture into the bowl of potatoes. Crumble bacon into the bowl, and stir to distribute. Serve.

CABBAGE JAMBALAYA

Servings: 6 | Prep: 20m | Cooks: 45m | Total: 1h5m

NUTRITION FACTS

Calories: 549 | Carbohydrates: 44.5g | Fat: 28.6g | Protein: 28.5g | Cholesterol: 96mg

INGREDIENTS

- 1 pound ground beef
- 1 medium head cabbage, chopped
- 1 pound smoked sausage, cut into 1/4-inch slices
- 1 (14.5 ounce) can stewed tomatoes
- 1 onion, chopped
- 141/2 fluid ounces water
- 3 stalks celery, chopped
- 1 cup uncooked rice
- 1 clove garlic, chopped
- 1 pinch garlic salt, or to taste

DIRECTIONS

1. Combine ground beef, smoked sausage, onion, celery, and garlic in a large stock pot over medium-high heat. Cook and stir until beef is evenly browned, about 5 minutes. Stir in cabbage, tomatoes, water, and rice. Season with garlic salt.
2. Bring to a boil; reduce heat to low. Cover and cook, stirring once, until rice is tender, 35 to 40 minutes. Preheat the oven to.

ARKANSAS GREEN BEANS

Servings: 10 | Prep: 15m | Cooks: 40m | Total: 55m

NUTRITION FACTS

Calories: 146 | Carbohydrates: 15.9g | Fat: 7.4g | Protein: 4.3g | Cholesterol: 19mg

INGREDIENTS

- 5 (15 ounce) cans green beans, drained
- 1/4 cup butter, melted
- 7 slices bacon
- 7 teaspoons soy sauce
- 2/3 cup brown sugar
- 1 1/2 teaspoons garlic powder

DIRECTIONS

1. Preheat an oven to 350 degrees F (175 degrees C). Place the drained green beans in a 9x13 inch baking pan.
2. Cook bacon in a microwave on microwave-safe plate for 2 minutes until slightly cooked. Lay the bacon on top of the green beans.
3. Combine the brown sugar, melted butter, soy sauce, and garlic powder in a small bowl. Pour the butter mixture over the green beans and bacon. Bake uncovered in the preheated oven for 40 minutes.

SOUTHERN GREEN BEANS

Servings: 8 | Prep: 15m | Cooks: 25m | Total: 40m

NUTRITION FACTS

Calories: 189 | Carbohydrates: 25.9g | Fat: 7.4g | Protein: 6.7g | Cholesterol: 19mg

INGREDIENTS

- 6 slices bacon, chopped
- 1 large clove garlic, minced
- 3 tablespoons butter

- 1/4 cup chicken broth
- 1 red onion, chopped
- 1 1/2 teaspoons white balsamic vinegar
- 2 pounds fresh green beans, trimmed and snapped
- salt and pepper to taste
- 8 small new potatoes, diced

DIRECTIONS

1. Place the chopped bacon in a skillet, and cook over medium heat, stirring occasionally, until evenly browned, 8 to 10 minutes. Drain the bacon pieces on a paper towel-lined plate.
2. Melt the butter in a skillet with a lid over medium-low heat, and cook and stir the onion until translucent, about 5 minutes. Stir in the cooked bacon, green beans, potatoes, garlic, and chicken broth. Bring to a boil, cover, and simmer over low heat until the green beans are tender, about 10 minutes. Sprinkle with vinegar, salt, and pepper, and serve.

LOUISIANA SWEET POTATO PANCAKES

Servings: 8 | Prep: 10m | Cooks: 15m | Total: 45m

NUTRITION FACTS

Calories: 215 | Carbohydrates: 29.2g | Fat: 8.2g | Protein: 6.2g | Cholesterol: 65mg

INGREDIENTS

- 3/4 pound sweet potatoes
- 1/2 teaspoon ground nutmeg
- 1 1/2 cups all-purpose flour
- 2 eggs, beaten
- 3 1/2 teaspoons baking powder
- 1 1/2 cups milk
- 1 teaspoon salt
- 1/4 cup butter, melted

DIRECTIONS

1. Place sweet potatoes in a medium saucepan of boiling water, and cook until tender but firm, about 15 minutes. Drain, and immediately immerse in cold water to loosen skins. Drain, remove skins, chop, and mash.
2. In a medium bowl, sift together flour, baking powder, salt, and nutmeg. Mix mashed sweet potatoes, eggs, milk and butter in a separate medium bowl. Blend sweet potato mixture into the flour mixture to form a batter.
3. Preheat a lightly greased griddle over medium-high heat. Drop batter mixture onto the prepared griddle by heaping tablespoonfuls, and cook until golden brown, turning once with a spatula when the surface begins to bubble.

SWEET POTATO PIE

Servings: 8 | Prep: 20m | Cooks: 40m | Total: 1h

NUTRITION FACTS

Calories: 449 | Carbohydrates: 60.2g | Fat: 21.6g | Protein: 5.5g | Cholesterol: 82mg

INGREDIENTS

- 2 cups mashed sweet potatoes
- 1/2 teaspoon ground cinnamon
- 1/4 pound butter, softened
- 1/2 teaspoon ground nutmeg
- 2 eggs, separated
- 1/2 cup evaporated milk
- 1 cup packed brown sugar
- 1/4 cup white sugar
- 1/4 teaspoon salt
- 1 (9 inch) unbaked pie crust
- 1/2 teaspoon ground ginger

DIRECTIONS

1. Preheat oven to 400 degrees F (200 degrees C).
2. In a mixing bowl, combine the sweet potatoes, butter, egg yolks, brown sugar, salt, ginger, cinnamon, nutmeg and evaporated milk. Mix together well.
3. Beat egg whites until stiff peaks form; add 1/4 cup sugar and fold into sweet potato mixture.
4. Pour into pie shell and bake at 400 degrees F (200 degrees C) for 10 minutes. Reduce heat and bake at 350 degrees F (175 degrees C) for 30 minutes or until firm.

LOUISIANA SHRIMP CREOLE

Servings: 5 | Prep: 20m | Cooks: 25m | Total: 45m

NUTRITION FACTS

Calories: 193 | Carbohydrates: 14.3g | Fat: 8.1g | Protein: 16.8g | Cholesterol: 157mg

INGREDIENTS

- 1/2 cup finely diced onion
- 1 (14.5 ounce) can stewed tomatoes
- 1/2 cup chopped green bell pepper
- 1 (8 ounce) can tomato sauce
- 1/2 cup chopped celery

* 1 tablespoon Worcestershire sauce
* 2 cloves garlic, minced
* 1 teaspoon chili powder
* 3 tablespoons butter
* 1 dash hot pepper sauce
* 2 tablespoons cornstarch
* 1 dash hot pepper sauce

DIRECTIONS

1. In a 2 quart saucepan, melt butter or margarine over medium heat. Add onion, green pepper, celery, and garlic; cook until tender.
2. Mix in cornstarch. Stir in stewed tomatoes, tomato sauce, Worcestershire sauce, chili powder, and red pepper sauce. Bring to a boil, stirring frequently. Stir in shrimp, and cook for 5 minutes.

FRIED OKRA

Servings: 4 | Prep: 15m | Cooks: 15m | Total: 30m

NUTRITION FACTS

Calories: 394 | Carbohydrates: 29g | Fat: 29.2g | Protein: 4.7g | Cholesterol: 46mg

INGREDIENTS

* 10 pods okra, sliced in 1/4 inch pieces
* 1/4 teaspoon salt
* 1 egg, beaten
* 1/4 teaspoon ground black pepper
* 1 cup cornmeal
* 1/2 cup vegetable oil

DIRECTIONS

1. In a small bowl, soak okra in egg for 5 to 10 minutes. In a medium bowl, combine cornmeal, salt, and pepper.
2. Heat oil in a large skillet over medium-high heat. Dredge okra in the cornmeal mixture, coating evenly. Carefully place okra in hot oil; stir continuously. Reduce heat to medium when okra first starts to brown, and cook until golden. Drain on paper towels.

MARDI GRAS KING CAKE

Servings: 16 | Prep: 1h | Cooks: 30m | Total: 4h30m | Additional: 3h

NUTRITION FACTS

Calories: 418 | Carbohydrates: 68.7g | Fat: 13.4g | Protein: 7.2g | Cholesterol: 47mg

INGREDIENTS

- 1 cup milk
- 1 cup packed brown sugar
- 1/4 cup butter
- 1 tablespoon ground cinnamon
- 2 (.25 ounce) packages active dry yeast
- 2/3 cup chopped pecans
- 2/3 cup warm water (110 degrees F/45 degrees C)
- 1/2 cup all-purpose flour
- 1/2 cup white sugar
- 1/2 cup raisins
- 2 eggs
- 1/2 cup melted butter
- 1 1/2 teaspoons salt
- 1 cup confectioners' sugar
- 1/2 teaspoon freshly grated nutmeg
- 1 tablespoon water
- 5 1/2 cups all-purpose flour

DIRECTIONS

1. Scald milk, remove from heat and stir in 1/4 cup of butter. Allow mixture to cool to room temperature. In a large bowl, dissolve yeast in the warm water with 1 tablespoon of the white sugar. Let stand until creamy, about 10 minutes.
2. When yeast mixture is bubbling, add the cooled milk mixture. Whisk in the eggs. Stir in the remaining white sugar, salt and nutmeg. Beat the flour into the milk/egg mixture 1 cup at a time. When the dough has pulled together, turn it out onto a lightly floured surface and knead until smooth and elastic, about 8 to 10 minutes.
3. Lightly oil a large bowl, place the dough in the bowl and turn to coat with oil. Cover with a damp cloth or plastic wrap and let rise in a warm place until doubled in volume, about 2 hours. When risen, punch down and divide dough in half.
4. Preheat oven to 375 degrees F (190 degrees C). Grease 2 cookie sheets or line with parchment paper.
5. To Make Filling: Combine the brown sugar, ground cinnamon, chopped pecans, 1/2 cup flour and 1/2 cup raisins. Pour 1/2 cup melted butter over the cinnamon mixture and mix until crumbly.
6. Roll dough halves out into large rectangles (approximately 10x16 inches or so). Sprinkle the filling evenly over the dough and roll up each half tightly like a jelly roll, beginning at the wide side. Bring the ends of each roll together to form 2 oval shaped rings. Place each ring on a prepared cookie sheet. With scissors make cuts 1/3 of the way through the rings at 1 inch intervals. Let rise in a warm spot until doubled in size, about 45 minutes.
7. Bake in preheated oven for 30 minutes. Push the doll into the bottom of the cake. Frost while warm with the confectioners' sugar blended with 1 to 2 tablespoons of water.

BAKED CHICKEN WITH PEACHES

Servings: 8 | Prep: 15m | Cooks: 30m | Total: 45m

NUTRITION FACTS

Calories: 248 | Carbohydrates: 30.3g | Fat: 2.8g | Protein: 24.6g | Cholesterol: 67mg

INGREDIENTS

- 8 skinless, boneless chicken breast halves
- 1/8 teaspoon ground ginger
- 1 cup brown sugar
- 1/8 teaspoon ground cloves
- 4 fresh peaches - peeled, pitted, and sliced
- 2 tablespoons fresh lemon juice

DIRECTIONS

1. Preheat oven to 350 degrees F (175 degrees C). Lightly grease a 9x13 inch baking dish.
2. Place chicken in the prepared baking dish, and sprinkle with 1/2 cup of brown sugar. Place peach slices over chicken, then sprinkle with remaining 1/2 cup brown sugar, ginger, cloves, and lemon juice.
3. Bake for about 30 minutes in the preheated oven, basting often with juices, until chicken is cooked through and juices run clear.

SIMPLE GRILLED LAMB CHOPS

Servings: 6 | Prep: 10m | Cooks: 6m | Total: 2h16m

NUTRITION FACTS

Calories: 519 | Carbohydrates: 2.3g | Fat: 44.8g | Protein: 25g | Cholesterol: 112mg

INGREDIENTS

- 1/4 cup distilled white vinegar
- 1 onion, thinly sliced
- 2 teaspoons salt
- 2 tablespoons olive oil
- 1/2 teaspoon black pepper
- 2 pounds lamb chop
- 1 tablespoon minced garlic

DIRECTIONS

1. Mix together the vinegar, salt, pepper, garlic, onion, and olive oil in a large resealable bag until the salt has dissolved. Add lamb, toss until coated, and marinate in refrigerator for 2 hours.
2. Preheat an outdoor grill for medium-high heat.
3. Remove lamb from the marinade and leave any onions on that stick to the meat. Discard any remaining marinade. Wrap the exposed ends of the bones with aluminum foil to keep them from burning. Grill to desired doneness, about 3 minutes per side for medium. The chops may also be broiled in the oven about 5 minutes per side for medium.

DELICIOUS APPLE SAUC
Servings: 6 | Prep: 15m | Cooks: 30m | Total: 45m

NUTRITION FACTS

Calories: 152 | Carbohydrates: 39.9g | Fat: 0.2g | Protein: 0.4g | Cholesterol: 0mg

INGREDIENTS

- 2 apples - peeled, cored and shredded
- 1/4 cup water
- 1 teaspoon ground cinnamon
- 3 tablespoons brown sugar

DIRECTIONS

1. Place shredded apples in a medium saucepan over medium low heat. Sprinkle with cinnamon, then add water and cook until the apple bits become soft and mushy.
2. Stir in brown sugar and mix well; if desired, top with ice cream and serve.

SOUTHERN FRIED CHICKEN
Servings: 6 | Prep: 15m | Cooks: 20m | Total: 35m

NUTRITION FACTS

Calories: 491 | Carbohydrates: 16.1g | Fat: 32g | Protein: 32.8g | Cholesterol: 97mg

INGREDIENTS

- 1 (3 pound) whole chicken, cut into pieces
- ground black pepper to taste
- 1 cup all-purpose flour
- 1 teaspoon paprika
- salt to taste
- 1 quart vegetable oil for frying

DIRECTIONS

1. Season chicken pieces with salt, pepper, and paprika. Roll in flour.
2. Add 1/2 to 3/4 inch oil to a large, heavy skillet. Heat to approximately 365 degrees F (185 degrees C). Place chicken pieces in hot oil. Cover, and fry until golden, turning once, 15 to 20 minutes. Drain on paper towels.

SOUTHERN PEACH COBBLER

Servings: 8 | Prep: 10m | Cooks: 45m | Total: 1h

NUTRITION FACTS

Calories: 306 | Carbohydrates: 49.5g | Fat: 12.1g | Protein: 2.5g | Cholesterol: 32mg

INGREDIENTS

- 1/2 cup butter
- 3/4 cup milk
- 1 cup white sugar
- 1 (29 ounce) can sliced peaches in light syrup
- 3/4 cup self-rising flour

DIRECTIONS

1. Preheat oven to 350 degrees F (175 degrees C). Place butter in a deep 2 quart baking dish and place in oven to melt.
2. In a medium bowl, mix sugar and flour. Stir in milk, a little at a time, until wholly incorporated. Pour carefully over melted butter in dish. Spoon peaches and syrup over batter.
3. Bake in preheated oven 35 to 45 minutes, until crust is puffed and golden.

OVEN-FRIED CATFISH

Servings: 6 | Prep: 10m | Cooks: 15m | Total: 25m

NUTRITION FACTS

Calories: 207 | Carbohydrates: 11g | Fat: 9g | Protein: 19.4g | Cholesterol: 54mg

INGREDIENTS

- 1 1/2 pounds catfish fillets
- 1/2 teaspoon onion powder
- 1/2 cup yellow cornmeal
- 1/2 teaspoon garlic powder
- 1 teaspoon paprika
- 1/2 teaspoon ground black pepper
- 1 teaspoon dried thyme

- 1/2 cup skim milk
- 1 teaspoon salt
- cooking spray
- 1/2 teaspoon celery seed

DIRECTIONS

1. Preheat the oven to 425 degrees F (220 degrees C). Line a baking sheet with aluminum foil and coat with cooking spray.
2. In a shallow dish, stir together the cornmeal, paprika, thyme, salt, celery seed, onion powder, garlic powder, and pepper. Dip the catfish fillets in milk, then place them into the cornmeal mixture and coat liberally; place on the greased baking sheet. Coat the tops of the fillets with cooking spray until wet.
3. Bake for 15 minutes in the preheated oven, or until fish is easily flaked with a fork.

SHRIMP ETOUFFEE

Servings: 6 | Prep: 20m | Cooks: 25m | Total: 45m

NUTRITION FACTS

Calories: 195 | Carbohydrates: 9g | Fat: 11.2g | Protein: 14.8g | Cholesterol: 119mg

INGREDIENTS

- 1/4 cup margarine
- 3 tablespoons tomato paste
- 1/2 cup chopped onion
- 1 (10.75 ounce) can condensed cream of chicken soup
- 1/2 cup chopped green onion
- 1 pound cleaned shrimp
- 1/2 cup chopped green bell pepper
- salt to taste
- 4 cloves minced garlic
- 1/4 teaspoon hot pepper sauce to taste
- 1/2 cup celery, diced
- 1/4 teaspoon cayenne pepper
- 1/2 cup chopped fresh parsley

DIRECTIONS

1. In a 2 quart microwave safe dish, combine margarine, onion, green onion, bell pepper, garlic and celery. Heat on High settings for 8 to 9 minutes.
2. Stir in parsley, tomato paste, soup, shrimp, salt, hot pepper sauce and cayenne. Heat on High setting for 5 minutes. Stir and cook for another 5 minutes until mixture thickens. Serve over white rice.

SWEET POTATO POUND CAKE

Servings: 14 | Prep: 20m | Cooks: 1h20m | Total: 2h | Additional: 20m

NUTRITION FACTS

Calories: 409 | Carbohydrates: 64.8g | Fat: 14.9g | Protein: 5.3g | Cholesterol: 88mg

INGREDIENTS

- 1 cup butter, softened
- 1 teaspoon ground cinnamon
- 2 cups white sugar
- 1/2 teaspoon baking soda
- 2 cups cooked and mashed sweet potatoes
- 1/2 teaspoon ground nutmeg
- 1 teaspoon vanilla extract
- 1/4 teaspoon salt
- 4 eggs
- 1 cup sifted confectioners' sugar
- 3 cups all-purpose flour
- 5 teaspoons orange juice
- 2 teaspoons baking powder
- 2 tablespoons grated orange zest

DIRECTIONS

1. Preheat oven to 350 degrees F (175 degrees C). Grease and flour a 10-inch tube pan. Sift together flour, baking powder, cinnamon, baking soda, nutmeg and salt. Set aside.
2. In large mixing bowl, cream butter and sugar until light and fluffy. Add mashed sweet potatoes and vanilla. Beat until well blended. Add eggs, one at a time (the batter will look curdled). Add flour mixture to potato mixture. Beat on low until combined.
3. Pour batter into 10 inch tube pan. Bake at 350 degrees F (175 degrees C) for about 1 hour and 20 minutes, or until a wooden toothpick inserted into cake comes out clean. Cool cake for 20 minutes in the pan, then invert onto serving plate
4. To make the glaze: in a small bowl, combine confectioners sugar with 3 to 5 teaspoons orange juice to achieve drizzling consistency. Spoon over warm cake and sprinkle with orange zest if desired.

MOUNTAIN APPLE COBBLER

Servings: 8 | Prep: 20m | Cooks: 45m | Total: 1h5m

NUTRITION FACTS

Calories: 613 | Carbohydrates: 72g | Fat: 35g | Protein: 4.4g | Cholesterol: 61mg

INGREDIENTS

- 2 (8 ounce) cans refrigerated crescent rolls
- 1 1/2 cups white sugar
- 2 large Granny Smith apples - peeled, cored, and cut into 8 wedges each
- 1 tablespoon ground cinnamon
- 1 cup butter, melted
- 1 (12 fluid ounce) can or bottle caffeinated citrus-flavored soda (such as Mountain Dew)

DIRECTIONS

1. Preheat oven to 350 degrees F (175 degrees C). Grease a 9x13 inch baking dish.
2. Unroll the crescent roll dough, and separate the sheets into individual triangles. Roll each apple wedge into a triangle of dough, and place them into the baking dish, seam sides down.
3. Mix the melted butter, sugar, and cinnamon in a bowl, and spoon evenly over the dough-wrapped apple slices. Pour the soda over the rolls.
4. Bake in the preheated oven until the top is browned, the apples are cooked through, and the cobbler is bubbling, 45 to 50 minutes.

MONTE CRISTO SANDWICH - THE REAL ONE

Servings: 8 | Prep: 10m | Cooks: 5m | Total: 15m

NUTRITION FACTS

Calories: 305 | Carbohydrates: 23.7g | Fat: 17.9g | Protein: 12.2g | Cholesterol: 50mg

INGREDIENTS

- 1 quart oil for frying, or as needed
- 8 slices white bread
- 2/3 cup water
- 4 slices Swiss cheese
- 1 egg
- 4 slices turkey
- 2/3 cup all-purpose flour
- 4 slices ham
- 1 3/4 teaspoons baking powder
- 1/8 teaspoon ground black pepper
- 1/2 teaspoon salt
- 1 tablespoon confectioners' sugar for dusting

DIRECTIONS

1. Heat 5 inches of oil in a deep-fryer to 365 degrees F (180 degrees C). While oil is heating, make the batter: In a medium bowl, whisk together the egg and water. Combine the flour, baking powder, salt and pepper; whisk into the egg mixture until smooth. Set aside in the refrigerator.
2. Assemble sandwiches by placing one slice of turkey on one slice of bread, a slice of ham on another, then sandwich them with the Swiss cheese in the middle. Cut sandwiches into quarters, and secure with toothpicks.
3. Dip each sandwich quarter in the batter so that all sides are coated. Deep fry in the hot oil until golden brown on all sides. Remove toothpicks and arrange on a serving tray. Dust with confectioners' sugar just before serving.

BIG ED'S CAJUN SHRIMP SOUP

Servings: 6 | Prep: 15m | Cooks: 25m | Total: 40m

NUTRITION FACTS

Calories: 163 | Carbohydrates: 19.6g | Fat: 3.2g | Protein: 13.8g | Cholesterol: 92mg

INGREDIENTS

- 1 tablespoon butter
- 1/4 teaspoon dried basil
- 1/2 cup chopped green bell pepper
- 1/4 teaspoon red pepper flakes
- 1/4 cup sliced green onions
- 1 bay leaf
- 1 clove garlic, minced
- 1/2 teaspoon salt
- 3 cups tomato-vegetable juice cocktail
- 1/2 cup uncooked long-grain white rice
- 1 (8 ounce) bottle clam juice
- 3/4 pound fresh shrimp, peeled and deveined
- 1/2 cup water
- hot pepper sauce to taste
- 1/4 teaspoon dried thyme

DIRECTIONS

1. Melt butter in a large pot over medium heat. Saute green bell pepper, onions, and garlic until tender. Stir in vegetable juice, clam juice, and water. Season with thyme, basil, red pepper, bay leaf, and salt. Bring to a boil, and stir in rice. Reduce heat, and cover. Simmer 15 minutes, until rice is tender.
2. Stir in shrimp, and cook 5 minutes, or until shrimp are opaque. Remove the bay leaf, and season with hot sauce.

BEIGNETS

Servings: 10 | Prep: 30m | Cooks: 30m | Total: 3h

NUTRITION FACTS

Calories: 543 | Carbohydrates: 82.7g | Fat: 17.7g | Protein: 12.4g | Cholesterol: 45mg

INGREDIENTS

- 2 1/4 teaspoons active dry yeast
- 1 cup evaporated milk
- 1 1/2 cups warm water (110 degrees F/45 degrees C)
- 7 cups all-purpose flour
- 1/2 cup white sugar
- 1/4 cup shortening
- 1 teaspoon salt
- 1 quart vegetable oil for frying
- 2 eggs
- 1/4 cup confectioners' sugar

DIRECTIONS

1. In a large bowl, dissolve yeast in warm water. Add sugar, salt, eggs, evaporated milk, and blend well. Mix in 4 cups of the flour and beat until smooth. Add the shortening, and then the remaining 3 cups of flour. Cover and chill for up to 24 hours. Watch Now
2. Roll out dough 1/8 inch thick. Cut into 2 1/2 inch squares. Fry in 360 degree F (180 degrees C) hot oil. If beignets do not pop up, oil is not hot enough. Drain onto paper towels. Watch Now
3. Shake confectioners' sugar on hot beignets. Serve warm. Watch Now.

HONEY CRUNCH PECAN PIE

Servings: 8 | Prep: 30m | Cooks: 1h | Total: 1h20m | Additional: 1h20m

NUTRITION FACTS

Calories: 848 | Carbohydrates: 88.8g | Fat: 53.6g | Protein: 9.6g | Cholesterol: 112mg

INGREDIENTS

- 2 cups all-purpose flour
- 1 cup light corn syrup
- 1 teaspoon salt
- 2 tablespoons butter, melted
- 3/4 cup shortening
- 1 teaspoon vanilla extract

- 6 tablespoons cold water
- 1 cup chopped pecans
- 1 teaspoon distilled white vinegar
- 1 tablespoon bourbon (optional)
- 4 eggs, lightly beaten
- 1/3 cup packed brown sugar
- 1/4 cup packed brown sugar
- 3 tablespoons butter
- 1/4 cup white sugar
- 3 tablespoons honey
- 1/2 teaspoon salt
- 1 1/2 cups pecan halves

DIRECTIONS

1. Preheat oven to 350 degrees F (175 degrees C).
2. To Make Crust: In a medium bowl, mix together flour and 1 teaspoon salt. Cut in shortening until mixture is crumbly. Gradually add water and vinegar. Cut together until mixture will hold together. Press dough into a ball and flour each side lightly. Wrap in plastic and chill for 20 minutes. Roll out between wax paper into a circle 1/8 inch thick and press into 9 inch pie pan.
3. To Make Filling: In a large bowl, combine eggs, 1/4 cup brown sugar, white sugar, 1/2 teaspoon salt, corn syrup, melted butter, vanilla extract, and chopped pecans. Add bourbon if desired. Mix well. Spoon mixture into unbaked pie shell.
4. Bake in preheated oven for 15 minutes. Remove and cover edges of pastry with aluminum foil. Return to oven for 20 minutes
5. To Make Topping: Combine 1/3 cup brown sugar, butter or margarine, and honey in a medium saucepan. Cook over low heat, stirring occasionally, until sugar dissolves - about 2 minutes. Add pecans. Stir just until coated. Spoon topping evenly over pie.
6. Keep foil on edges of pastry and return pie to oven for an additional 10 to 20 minutes, until topping is bubbly and golden brown. Cool to room temperature before serving.

SOUTHERN GRILLED BARBECUED RIBS

Servings: 8 | Prep: 20m | Cooks: 1h30m | Total: 1h50m

NUTRITION FACTS

Calories: 519 | Carbohydrates: 24.5g | Fat: 35.5g | Protein: 25g | Cholesterol: 132mg

INGREDIENTS

- 4 pounds baby back pork ribs
- 1/3 cup Worcestershire sauce
- 2/3 cup water

- 1/4 cup prepared mustard
- 1/3 cup red wine vinegar
- 4 tablespoons butter
- 1 cup ketchup
- 1/2 cup packed brown sugar
- 1 cup water
- 1 teaspoon hot pepper sauce
- 1/2 cup cider vinegar
- 1/8 teaspoon salt

DIRECTIONS

1. Preheat oven to 350 degrees F (175 degrees C). Place ribs in two 10x15 inch roasting pans. Pour water and red wine vinegar into a bowl, and stir. Pour diluted vinegar over ribs and cover with foil. Bake in the preheated oven for 45 minutes. Baste the ribs with their juices halfway through cooking.
2. In a medium saucepan, mix together ketchup, water, vinegar, Worcestershire sauce, mustard, butter, brown sugar, hot pepper sauce, and salt; bring to a boil. Reduce heat to low, cover, and simmer barbeque sauce for 1 hour.
3. Preheat grill for medium heat.
4. Lightly oil preheated grill. Transfer ribs from the oven to the grill, discarding cooking liquid. Grill over medium heat for 15 minutes, turning ribs once. Baste ribs generously with barbeque sauce, and grill 8 minutes. Turn ribs, baste again with barbeque sauce, and grill 8 minutes.

CRAWFISH CHOWDER

Servings: 10 | Prep: 20m | Cooks: 25m | Total: 45m

NUTRITION FACTS

Calories: 395 | Carbohydrates: 20.6g | Fat: 27.5g | Protein: 17.7g | Cholesterol: 167mg

INGREDIENTS

- 1/4 cup butter
- 1 (10.75 ounce) can condensed cream of mushroom soup
- 1/2 bunch green onions, chopped
- 1 (15.25 ounce) can whole kernel corn, drained
- 1/2 cup butter
- 4 ounces cream cheese, softened
- 2 pounds frozen crawfish, cleaned
- 2 cups half-and-half cream
- 2 (10.75 ounce) cans condensed cream of potato soup
- 1/2 teaspoon cayenne pepper

DIRECTIONS

1. Melt 1/4 cup of butter in a large skillet over medium heat. Saute green onions in butter until tender. Remove from pan, and set aside. In the same skillet, melt 1/2 cup of butter, and saute the crawfish for 5 minutes; set aside.
2. In a large pot over medium heat, combine potato soup, mushroom soup, corn, and cream cheese. Mix well, and bring to a slow boil. Stir in half-and-half, sauteed green onions, and crawfish. Season with cayenne pepper. Bring to a low boil, and simmer 5 minutes to blend flavors.

SOUTHERN AS YOU CAN GET COLLARD GREENS
Servings: 8 | Prep: 15m | Cooks: 1h | Total: 1h15m

NUTRITION FACTS

Calories: 165 | Carbohydrates: 2.6g | Fat: 11.4g | Protein: 12.7g | Cholesterol: 35mg

INGREDIENTS

- 1 bunch collard greens - rinsed, trimmed and chopped
- 21 fluid ounces water
- 2 smoked ham hocks
- 1 tablespoon distilled white vinegar
- 2 (10.5 ounce) cans condensed chicken broth
- salt and pepper to taste

DIRECTIONS

1. Place the collard greens and ham hocks in a large pot. Mix in the chicken broth, water, and vinegar. Season with salt and pepper. Bring to a boil, reduce heat to low, and simmer 1 hour.

SOUTHERN BAKED YELLOW SQUASH
Servings: 10 | Prep: 20m | Cooks: 1h15m | Total: 1h35m

NUTRITION FACTS

Calories: 162 | Carbohydrates: 13.5g | Fat: 11g | Protein: 3.8g | Cholesterol: 62mg

INGREDIENTS

- 3 pounds yellow summer squash, cut into 1-inch cubes
- 1 tablespoon white sugar
- 1/2 cup dry bread crumbs
- 1 teaspoon salt
- 1/2 cup chopped onion

- 1/2 teaspoon black pepper
- 2 eggs
- 1/4 cup butter, melted
- 1/4 cup butter, melted
- 1/4 cup dry bread crumbs

DIRECTIONS

1. Preheat an oven to 375 degrees F (190 degrees C). Grease a 2-quart baking dish.
2. Place the squash in a large saucepan, cover with water, and boil until soft, about 15 minutes. Drain the squash well, place in a large mixing bowl, and mash until slightly chunky. Stir in 1/2 cup of bread crumbs, onion, eggs, 1/4 cup of butter, sugar, salt, and pepper until thoroughly combined, and spread mixture into the prepared baking dish. Drizzle the top of the casserole with 1/4 cup melted butter, and sprinkle 1/4 cup bread crumbs over the butter.
3. Bake in the preheated oven until the casserole is cooked through and the top is golden brown, about 1 hour.

CHESS PIE

Servings: 8 | Prep: 15m | Cooks: 50m | Total: 1h5m

NUTRITION FACTS

Calories: 460 | Carbohydrates: 62g | Fat: 22.1g | Protein: 5.3g | Cholesterol: 126mg

INGREDIENTS

- 1/2 cup butter
- 1 tablespoon cornmeal
- 2 cups white sugar
- 1/4 cup evaporated milk
- 1 teaspoon vanilla extract
- 1 tablespoon distilled white vinegar
- 4 eggs
- 1 (9 inch) unbaked pie shell

DIRECTIONS

1. Preheat the oven to 425 degrees F (220 degrees C).
2. In a large bowl, mix the butter, sugar and vanilla together. Mix in the eggs, then stir in the cornmeal, evaporated milk and vinegar until smooth.
3. Bake for 10 minutes in the preheated oven, then reduce heat to 300 degrees F (150 degrees C) for 40 minutes. Let cool. Cut and top servings with whipped cream. You will think you have died and gone to heaven.

ELAINE'S SWEET AND TANGY LOOSE BEEF BBQ

Servings: 24 | Prep: 15m | Cooks: 8h | Total: 8h30m

NUTRITION FACTS

Calories: 231 | Carbohydrates: 10.7g | Fat: 13.7g | Protein: 16.3g | Cholesterol: 60mg

INGREDIENTS

- 7 pounds boneless chuck roast
- 3 cups ketchup
- 1 cup water
- 2 teaspoons salt
- 3 tablespoons white vinegar
- 3/4 teaspoon ground black pepper
- 4 tablespoons brown sugar
- 1/4 teaspoon cayenne pepper
- 2 teaspoons dry mustard
- 6 cloves garlic, minced
- 4 tablespoons Worcestershire sauce

DIRECTIONS

1. Place the roast into a slow cooker along with the water. Cover, and cook on LOW for 2 to 4 hours, or until beef can be easily shredded with a fork.
2. Shred the beef, removing fat as you go. Remove 1/2 cup of the broth from the slow cooker, and reserve for later. Add the vinegar, brown sugar, dry mustard, Worcestershire sauce and ketchup. Mix in the salt, pepper, cayenne, and garlic. Stir so that the meat is well coated.
3. Cover, and continue to cook beef on LOW for an additional 4 to 6 hours. Add the reserved broth only if necessary to maintain moisture. Serve on toasted buns. The meat can be frozen for future use.

GRILLED BUFFALO WINGS

Servings: 8 | Prep: 15m | Cooks: 50m | Total: 1h5m

NUTRITION FACTS

Calories: 129 | Carbohydrates: 5.5g | Fat: 7.3g | Protein: 10g | Cholesterol: 30mg

INGREDIENTS

- 3 pounds chicken wings, separated at joints, tips discarded
- 1/4 teaspoon cayenne pepper, or to taste
- 1 cup Louisiana-style hot sauce
- 1/4 teaspoon ground black pepper, or to taste

- 1 (12 fluid ounce) can or bottle cola-flavored carbonated beverage
- 1 tablespoon soy sauce

DIRECTIONS

1. Preheat a grill to medium heat.
2. In a large pot, mix together the hot sauce, cola, cayenne pepper, black pepper and soy sauce. Add the wings to the sauce - frozen is okay. Place the pot to one side of the grill, so the sauce comes to a simmer.
3. Use tongs to fish wings out of the sauce, and place them on the grill for 8 to 10 minutes. Then return to the sauce to simmer. Repeat this process for about 50 minutes. The sauce will thicken. When the chicken is tender and pulls easily off of the bone, you have two options. You can dip one last time and serve for sloppy style wings, or serve right off the grill for dryer wings.

SLOW-COOKED GREEN BEANS

Servings: 6 | Prep: 15m | Cooks: 2h10m | Total: 2h25m

NUTRITION FACTS

Calories: 124 | Carbohydrates: 16g | Fat: 4.3g | Protein: 7.3g | Cholesterol: 13mg

INGREDIENTS

- 6 slices bacon, sliced crosswise into 1/2-inch pieces
- 2 pounds fresh green beans, trimmed
- 1 onion, sliced lengthwise
- 3 cups chicken broth
- 3 cloves garlic, minced
- salt and ground black pepper to taste
- 1/4 cup tomato sauce
- 1 pinch cayenne pepper, or to taste

DIRECTIONS

1. Place saucepan over medium heat; cook and stir bacon in the hot pan until almost crisp, about 6 minutes. Add onion; cook until browned bits of food on the bottom of the pan have dissolved in the onion's juices and onion is soft and golden brown, about 5 minutes. Stir in garlic and tomato sauce. Cook until garlic has softened, about 1 more minute.
2. Place green beans into a skillet and pour in chicken broth. Raise heat to high, add salt, black pepper, and cayenne pepper to beans, and bring to a simmer. Beans will begin to soften. Turn heat to medium-low and simmer for 1 1/2 hours. Stir occasionally. Add more broth or water if mixture seems dry.
3. Adjust levels of salt, black pepper, and cayenne pepper to taste. Cook until beans are soft and tender, about 30 more minutes. Transfer beans and some of the pan juices to a deep serving platter.

GROUND BEEF AND CABBAGE

Servings: 6 | Prep: 15m | Cooks: 45m | Total: 1h

NUTRITION FACTS

Calories: 228 | Carbohydrates: 18.3g | Fat: 9.5g | Protein: 18.1g | Cholesterol: 50mg

INGREDIENTS

- 1 large head cabbage, finely chopped
- 1 tablespoon Italian seasoning
- 1 (14.5 ounce) can diced tomatoes with juice
- salt and ground black pepper to taste
- 1 onion, halved and thinly sliced
- 1 pound lean ground beef

DIRECTIONS

1. Combine cabbage, tomatoes with juice, onion, Italian seasoning, salt, and black pepper in a large pot over low heat. Bring cabbage mixture to a simmer and crumble ground beef into the pot. Cover and cook until cabbage is tender and ground beef is cooked through, about 45 minutes. Stir occasionally.

CHOCOLATE GRAVY

Servings: 8 | Prep: 5m | Cooks: 15m | Total: 20m

NUTRITION FACTS

Calories: 225 | Carbohydrates: 26.1g | Fat: 13.1g | Protein: 3.1g | Cholesterol: 35mg

INGREDIENTS

- 1/2 cup butter
- 3/4 cup white sugar
- 4 tablespoons unsweetened cocoa powder
- 2 cups milk
- 1/4 cup all-purpose flour

DIRECTIONS

1. Melt butter in a skillet over medium heat. Add cocoa and flour; stir until a thick paste is formed. Stir in sugar and milk. Cook, stirring constantly, until thick.

SWEET AND SAVORY SLOW COOKER PULLED PORK

Servings: 10 | Prep: 20m | Cooks: 6h15m | Total: 15h5m | Additional: 8h30m

NUTRITION FACTS

Calories: 485 | Carbohydrates: 45.5g | Fat: 19.1g | Protein: 28.5g | Cholesterol: 81mg

INGREDIENTS

- 1 (4.5 pound) bone-in pork shoulder roast
- 1/4 teaspoon ground cinnamon
- 1 cup root beer
- 1/4 teaspoon ground ginger
- 2 1/2 tablespoons light brown sugar
- 1/4 teaspoon ground nutmeg
- 2 teaspoons kosher salt
- 1/3 cup balsamic vinegar
- 1/2 teaspoon ground black pepper
- 11/2 cups root beer
- 11/2 teaspoons ground paprika
- 11/2 fluid ounces whiskey
- 1/2 teaspoon dry mustard
- 1/4 cup brown sugar
- 1/2 teaspoon onion powder
- 1 tablespoon olive oil
- 1/4 teaspoon garlic salt
- 3/4 cup prepared barbecue sauce
- 1/4 teaspoon celery salt
- 10 hamburger buns, split

DIRECTIONS

1. Place the pork shoulder roast into a large plastic bag, pour 1 cup of root beer over the meat, and squeeze out all the air from the bag. Seal the bag closed, and refrigerate 6 hours to overnight.
2. The next day, mix together the light brown sugar, kosher salt, black pepper, paprika, dry mustard, onion powder, garlic salt, celery salt, cinnamon, ginger, and nutmeg in a bowl.
3. Remove the meat from the marinade, and shake off the excess. Rub the meat all over with the spice mixture, wrap in plastic wrap, and refrigerate for 30 minutes to 2 hours.
4. Mix together the balsamic vinegar, 1 1/2 cups of root beer, whiskey, and brown sugar in a bowl, and stir until the sugar dissolves.
5. Heat the olive oil in a skillet over medium-high heat, and sear the meat on all sides until the meat develops a brown crust, about 3 minutes per side. Place the seared meat into a slow cooker. Pour the balsamic vinegar-root beer mixture over the meat, set the slow cooker to High, and cook for 6 to 8 hours.
6. Remove the roast from the slow cooker, and shred with 2 forks. Discard the bones and all but 1 cup of the liquid in the slow cooker. Return the shredded meat to the cooker, mix in the barbecue sauce, and let sit on Low until ready to serve. Serve piled on buns.

SOUTHERN DILL POTATO SALAD

Servings: 8 | Prep: 20m | Cooks: 20m | Total: 1h10m

NUTRITION FACTS

Calories: 279 | Carbohydrates: 10.8g | Fat: 24.1g | Protein: 5.9g | Cholesterol: 134mg

INGREDIENTS

- 10 unpeeled red potatoes
- 1/2 white onion, finely chopped
- 5 hard boiled eggs, roughly chopped
- 1 stalk celery, finely chopped
- 3/4 cup sour cream
- 1 teaspoon celery salt
- 3/4 cup mayonnaise
- salt and black pepper to taste
- 1 tablespoon apple cider vinegar, or to taste
- 1 tablespoon dried dill weed
- 1 tablespoon Dijon mustard, or to taste

DIRECTIONS

1. Place the potatoes in a large pot, cover them with water, and bring to a boil over high heat. Reduce the heat to medium-low, and simmer until the potatoes are cooked through but still firm, about 20 minutes. Remove from the water, let cool, and cut the potatoes into chunks. Set the potatoes aside.
2. In a bowl, stir together the sour cream, mayonnaise, apple cider vinegar, Dijon mustard, onion, celery, celery salt, and salt and pepper until well mixed.
3. Place the potatoes and eggs in a large salad bowl, and sprinkle with dried dill. Pour the dressing over the potatoes and eggs, and mix lightly. Cover and refrigerate the salad for at least 30 minutes. Serve cold.

DEEP SOUTH FRIED CHICKEN

Servings: 8 | Prep: 10m | Cooks: 35m | Total: 45m

NUTRITION FACTS

Calories: 351 | Carbohydrates: 26.5g | Fat: 14.7g | Protein: 26g | Cholesterol: 72mg

INGREDIENTS

- 1 cup shortening
- 1 teaspoon ground black pepper
- 2 cups all-purpose flour
- 1 (2 to 3 pound) whole chicken, cut into piece

- 1 teaspoon salt

DIRECTIONS

1. Heat the shortening in a large, cast iron skillet over medium-high heat.
2. In a brown paper lunch bag, combine the flour, salt, and pepper. Shake two chicken pieces in the bag to coat, and place them in the skillet. Repeat until all of the chicken is coated and in the skillet.
3. Fry the chicken over medium-high heat until all of the pieces have been browned on both sides. Turn the heat to medium-low, cover, and cook for 25 minutes. Remove the lid, and increase heat to medium-high. Continue frying until chicken pieces are a deep golden brown, and the juices run clear.

KENTUCKY PECAN PIE

Servings: 8 | Prep: 15m | Cooks: 1h | Total: 1h15m

NUTRITION FACTS

Calories: 523 | Carbohydrates: 70.8g | Fat: 26.8g | Protein: 5.1g | Cholesterol: 90mg

INGREDIENTS

- 1 cup white corn syrup
- 3 eggs
- 1 cup packed brown sugar
- 1 cup chopped pecans
- 1/2 teaspoon salt
- 1 recipe pastry for a 9 inch single crust pie
- 1/3 cup butter, melted

DIRECTIONS

1. Combine syrup, sugar, salt, and melted butter or margarine. Slightly beat the eggs, and add to sugar mixture. Beat well, and pour into uncooked pie shell. Sprinkle pecans on top.
2. Bake at 350 degrees F (175 degrees C) for 50 to 60 minutes.

BUTTERMILK CHESS PIE

Servings: 8 | Prep: 30m | Cooks: 45m | Total: 2h15m | Additional: 1h

NUTRITION FACTS

Calories: 470 | Carbohydrates: 63g | Fat: 22.3g | Protein: 6.3g | Cholesterol: 148mg

INGREDIENTS

- 2 cups white sugar
- 1/2 cup melted butter
- 2 tablespoons all-purpose flour
- 1 teaspoon vanilla extract
- 5 eggs
- 1 (9 inch) unbaked pie crust
- 2/3 cup buttermilk

DIRECTIONS

1. Preheat oven to 350 degrees F (175 degrees C.)
2. In a large bowl, combine sugar and flour. Beat in the eggs and buttermilk until blended. Stir in the melted butter and vanilla. Pour filling into the pie crust.
3. Bake in the preheated oven until filling is set, about 45 minutes.

REMOULADE SAUCE A LA NEW ORLEANS

Servings: 6 | Prep: 20m | Cooks: 0m | Total: 20m

NUTRITION FACTS

Calories: 359 | Carbohydrates: 6.7g | Fat: 37.3g | Protein: 1g | Cholesterol: 14mg

INGREDIENTS

- 1 cup mayonnaise
- 2 tablespoons chopped fresh parsley
- 1/4 cup chili sauce
- 2 tablespoons chopped green olives
- 2 tablespoons Creole mustard
- 2 tablespoons minced celery
- 2 tablespoons extra-virgin olive oil
- 1 clove garlic, minced
- 1 tablespoon Louisiana-style hot sauce, or to taste
- 1/2 teaspoon chili powder
- 2 tablespoons fresh lemon juice
- 1 teaspoon salt, or to taste
- 1 teaspoon Worcestershire sauce
- 1/2 teaspoon ground black pepper
- 4 medium scallions, chopped
- 1 teaspoon capers, chopped (optional)

DIRECTIONS

1. Mix together mayonnaise, chili sauce, mustard, olive oil, hot sauce, lemon juice, and Worcestershire sauce. Stir in scallions, parsley, olives, celery, capers, and garlic. Season with chili powder, and salt and pepper. Cover, and refrigerate.

SOUTHERN HAM AND BROWN BEANS

Servings: 8 | Prep: 10m | Cooks: 3h | Total: 3h10m

NUTRITION FACTS

Calories: 272 | Carbohydrates: 37.7g | Fat: 6g | Protein: 16.7g | Cholesterol: 17mg

INGREDIENTS

- 1 pound dry pinto beans
- 2 cloves garlic, minced
- 8 cups water
- 1 teaspoon chili powder
- 1 large, meaty ham hock
- 1 teaspoon salt, or to taste
- 1 large onion, chopped
- 1/4 teaspoon ground black pepper, or to taste

DIRECTIONS

1. Place the beans and water in a large stockpot. Add the ham hock, onion and garlic. Season with chili powder, salt and pepper. Bring to a boil, and cook for 2 minutes. Cover, and remove from heat. Let stand for one hour.
2. Return the pot to the heat, and bring to a boil once again. Reduce heat to medium-low, and simmer for at least 3 hours to blend flavors. The longer you simmer, the thicker the broth will become. I like to cook mine for about 6 hours.
3. Remove the ham hock from the broth, and let cool. Remove the meat from the bone, and return the meat to the stockpot, discarding the bone. Adjust seasonings to taste.

COSTAS FRENCH MARKET DOUGHNUTS (BEIGNETS)

Servings: 12 | Prep: 30m | Cooks: 30m | Total: 1h30m

NUTRITION FACTS

Calories: 503 | Carbohydrates: 80.9g | Fat: 14.8g | Protein: 10.9g | Cholesterol: 37mg

INGREDIENTS

- 1/2 cup water
- 1 cup evaporated milk

- 1 tablespoon yeast
- 2 eggs, beaten
- 1/4 cup shortening
- 7 1/2 cups flour
- 1/2 cup sugar
- 1 quart vegetable oil for frying
- 1 teaspoon salt
- 1 cup confectioners' sugar for dusting
- 1 cup boiling water
- 1 cup evaporated milk

DIRECTIONS

1. Pour 1/2 cup room temperature water into a small bowl. Sprinkle the yeast over the water and let stand for about 5 minutes to dissolve.
2. Combine the shortening, sugar, and salt in a large bowl. Pour the boiling water over the shortening mixture and then stir in the evaporated milk. Wait for the mixture to cool down until it is lukewarm. Then, add the yeast and water mixture and beaten eggs.
3. Slowly mix in the flour until the dough forms a ball. Cover the dough with plastic wrap and refrigerate for 30 minutes to 1 hour.
4. Working with a small portion (a little larger than a baseball) at a time, roll out the dough 1/8-inch thick. Cut the rolled out dough into strips 2 to 3-inches wide, then cut again in the opposite direction and at an angle, making diamond shapes.
5. Heat your oil for frying in a deep and wide, heavy-bottomed skillet over medium-high heat to 360 degree F (180 degrees C).
6. Slide dough slowly into the oil to avoid splattering and deep fry until they puff up and are golden brown, 3 to 5 minutes. Carefully remove onto a rack with paper towels underneath and allow to cool until you can handle them. Place in a clean paper bag with confectioners' sugar and shake gently until covered generously or, use a sifter to dust the beignets with powdered sugar.

SPICY GARLIC AND PEPPER SHRIMP

Servings: 1 | Prep: 25m | Cooks: 10m | Total: 35m

NUTRITION FACTS

Calories: 406 | Carbohydrates: 12.1g | Fat: 35.6g | Protein: 12.3g | Cholesterol: 85mg

INGREDIENTS

- 2 1/2 tablespoons vegetable oil
- 2 teaspoons crushed red pepper flakes
- 1/4 cup water
- 2 tablespoons sliced onion
- 1 cup shredded cabbage
- 1 tablespoon chopped fresh cilantro

- 1 tablespoon minced garlic
- 1 tablespoon soy sauce
- 8 large fresh shrimp, peeled and deveined

DIRECTIONS

1. Heat 1 tablespoon oil in a skillet over high heat. Add cabbage and 1 tablespoon water stir-fry for 30 seconds. Remove cabbage from skillet and place on a serving platter.
2. Heat the remaining 1 1/2 tablespoons oil in the skillet over high heat. Place the garlic and shrimp in the skillet and stir until garlic is lightly browned and shrimp turns pink. Add pepper, onion, cilantro, soy sauce and remaining water to the skillet. Stir-fry for 10 seconds. Pour the hot mixture onto the cabbage.

JAMBALAYA

Servings: 8 | Prep: 30m | Cooks: 1h30m | Total: 2h

NUTRITION FACTS

Calories: 556 | Carbohydrates: 35.3g | Fat: 28.7g | Protein: 37g | Cholesterol: 101mg

INGREDIENTS

- 1 (2 to 3 pound) whole chicken, cut into pieces
- 1/2 teaspoon hot pepper sauce
- 1 pound smoked sausage, sliced
- 1/2 teaspoon ground cayenne pepper
- 3 green bell peppers, diced
- 1 teaspoon Worcestershire sauce
- 2 onions, diced
- 5 bay leaves
- 5 cloves garlic, minced
- 1 (6 ounce) can tomato paste
- 2 (14.5 ounce) cans peeled and diced tomatoes
- 1 cup uncooked white rice
- 1 tablespoon chili powder

DIRECTIONS

1. Place chicken and sausage in a large pot and cover with water. Bring to a boil, then reduce heat and simmer until chicken is opaque and falls from the bone, 45 minutes. (I usually do this the night before and refrigerate to skim the fat.) Remove chicken and sausage, reserving broth. Shred chicken.
2. In a large pot over medium heat, cook bell pepper, onion and garlic until onion is translucent, adding reserved chicken broth if necessary. Stir in tomatoes, chili powder, pepper sauce, cayenne, Worcestershire and bay leaves; reduce heat and simmer 15 minutes.

3. Stir the shredded chicken, sausage and tomato paste into the spiced vegetables. Continue to simmer until flavor is as spicy as you like, adding reserved liquid as needed to thin.

4. Stir in 1 cup reserved liquid with the rice. Simmer 20 minutes, until rice is tender. Serve or continue to simmer, as desired.

CAJUN CRAB SOUP

Servings: 8 | Prep: 15m | Cooks: 30m | Total: 45m

NUTRITION FACTS

Calories: 420 | Carbohydrates: 14.5g | Fat: 34.6g | Protein: 15.1g | Cholesterol: 164mg

INGREDIENTS

- 1/2 cup unsalted butter
- 1 teaspoon salt
- 1 onion, chopped
- 1/2 teaspoon ground white pepper
- 2 cloves garlic, minced
- 1/4 teaspoon dried thyme
- 1/4 cup all-purpose flour
- 1/4 teaspoon ground cayenne pepper
- 2 cups clam juice
- 2 cups heavy cream
- 2 cups chicken broth
- 1 pound lump crabmeat, drained
- 1 (10 ounce) package frozen white corn
- 4 green onions, chopped

DIRECTIONS

1. Melt butter in a large saucepan over medium heat. Saute onion and garlic until onion is tender. Whisk in flour, and cook 2 minutes. Stir in clam juice and chicken broth, and bring to a boil. Mix in corn, and season with salt, white pepper, thyme, and cayenne. Reduce heat, and simmer 15 minutes.

2. Stir in cream, crab meat, and green onions. Heat through, but do not boil once the cream has been added.

CATFISH CAKES

Servings: 8 | Prep: 30m | Cooks: 15m | Total: 45m

NUTRITION FACTS

Calories: 481 | Carbohydrates: 42.9g | Fat: 27.7g | Protein: g13.8 | Cholesterol: 50mg

INGREDIENTS

- 1 pound catfish fillets
- 1/2 teaspoon Old Bay Seasoning TM, or to taste
- 1 medium onion, chopped
- 2 1/2 cups coarsely crushed buttery round crackers
- 1 teaspoon prepared yellow mustard
- 1 egg
- 1 tablespoon creamy salad dressing (e.g. Miracle Whip)
- 1 cup vegetable oil (for frying)

DIRECTIONS

1. Place catfish in a saucepan with enough water to cover. Bring to a boil, and cook until fish flakes easily with a fork. Drain off water, and mash up the fish. Stir in the onion, mustard, salad dressing, Old Bay(TM), cracker crumbs and egg. Mix until evenly blended.
2. Heat oil in a large heavy skillet over medium-high heat. Form the fish mixture into patties, and fry in the hot oil. Drain on paper towels, and serve hot.

SOUTHERN GRITS CASSEROLE

Servings: 16 | Prep: 15m | Cooks: 45m | Total: 1h

NUTRITION FACTS

Calories: 403 | Carbohydrates: 16.8g | Fat: 29.9g | Protein: 16.5g | Cholesterol: 202mg

INGREDIENTS

- 6 cups water
- 1 pound ground pork sausage
- 2 cups uncooked grits
- 12 eggs
- 1/2 cup butter, divided
- 1/2 cup milk
- 3 cups shredded Cheddar cheese, divided
- salt and pepper to taste

DIRECTIONS

1. Preheat oven to 350 degrees F (175 degrees C). Lightly grease a large baking dish.
2. Bring water to a boil in a large saucepan, and stir in grits. Reduce heat, cover, and simmer about 5 minutes, until liquid has been absorbed. Mix in 1/2 the butter and 2 cups cheese until melted.

3. In a skillet over medium-high heat, cook the sausage until evenly browned. Drain, and mix into the grits. Beat together the eggs and milk in a bowl, and pour into the skillet. Lightly scramble, then mix into the grits.
4. Pour the grits mixture into the prepared baking dish. Dot with remaining butter, and top with remaining cheese. Season with salt and pepper.
5. Bake 30 minutes in the preheated oven, until lightly browned.

AUTHENTIC CINCINNATI CHILI

Servings: 10 | Prep: 15m | Cooks: 3h30m | Total: 11h45m

NUTRITION FACTS

Calories: 225 | Carbohydrates: 10.1g | Fat: 12.6g | Protein: 19.1g | Cholesterol: 59mg

INGREDIENTS

- 2 pounds lean ground beef
- 1/4 cup chili powder
- 1 quart water, or amount to cover
- 1 1/2 teaspoons salt
- 2 onions, finely chopped
- 1 teaspoon ground cumin
- 1 (15 ounce) can tomato sauce
- 1 teaspoon ground cinnamon
- 2 tablespoons vinegar
- 1/2 teaspoon ground cayenne pepper
- 2 teaspoons Worcestershire sauce
- 5 whole cloves
- 4 cloves garlic, minced
- 5 whole allspice berries
- 1/2 (1 ounce) square unsweetened chocolate
- 1 bay leaf

DIRECTIONS

1. Place the ground beef in a large pan, cover with about 1 quart of cold water, and bring to a boil, stirring and breaking up the beef with a fork to a fine texture. Slowly boil until the meat is thoroughly cooked, about 30 minutes, then remove from heat and refrigerate in the pan overnight.
2. The next day, skim the solid fat from the top of the pan, and discard the fat. Place the beef mixture over medium heat, and stir in the onions, tomato sauce, vinegar, Worcestershire sauce, garlic, chocolate, chili powder, salt, cumin, cinnamon, cayenne pepper, cloves, allspice berries, and bay leaf. Bring to a boil, reduce heat to a simmer, and cook, stirring occasionally, for 3 hours. Add water if necessary to prevent the chili from burning.

OKLAHOMA CHEESE GRITS

Servings: 12 | Prep: 15m | Cooks: 1h11m | Total: 1h30m | Additional: 4m

NUTRITION FACTS

Calories: 258 | Carbohydrates: 6.1g | Fat: 22.3g | Protein: 8.9g | Cholesterol: 107mg

INGREDIENTS

- 6 cups water
- 1 tablespoon Worcestershire sauce
- 1 1/2 cups quick-cooking grits, dry
- 1/2 teaspoon hot pepper sauce
- 3/4 cup butter
- 2 teaspoons salt
- 1 pound processed cheese, cubed
- 3 eggs, beaten
- 2 teaspoons seasoning salt

DIRECTIONS

1. Preheat oven to 350 degrees F (175 degrees C). Lightly grease a 9x13 inch baking dish.
2. In a medium saucepan, bring the water to a boil. Stir in grits, and reduce heat to low. Cover, and cook 5 to 6 minutes, stirring occasionally. Mix in the butter, cheese, seasoning salt, Worcestershire sauce, hot pepper sauce, and salt. Continue cooking for 5 minutes, or until the cheese is melted. Remove from heat, cool slightly, and fold in the eggs. Pour into the prepared baking dish.
3. Bake 1 hour in the preheated oven, or until the top is lightly browned.

COUNTRY SAUSAGE GRAVY

Servings: 4 | Prep:15m | Cooks: 20m | Total: 35m

NUTRITION FACTS

Calories: 700 | Carbohydrates: 20.3g | Fat: 60.1g | Protein: 19.7g | Cholesterol: 118mg

INGREDIENTS

- 1 pound pork sausage
- 4 tablespoons all-purpose flour
- 1 onion, finely chopped
- 1 teaspoon minced fresh sage
- 1 green bell pepper, finely chopped
- 1 teaspoon minced fresh thyme
- 1 teaspoon crushed red pepper flakes

- 2 cups milk, divided
- 2 tablespoons garlic, minced
- 2 cubes chicken bouillon
- 4 tablespoons unsalted butter
- 1/4 cup minced fresh parsley
- salt and pepper to taste

DIRECTIONS

1. In a skillet on medium heat cook pork, onion, green pepper, red pepper flakes, and garlic until pork is crumbly. Drain off excess fat, but leave a small amount.
2. Combine butter, salt, and pepper with the meat mixture and stir until butter melts. Slowly sift flour over the top. Mix gently and allow mixture to cook for 5 minutes. It will burn, so do not let it sit unguarded. Don't forget to scrape the bottom of the pan. Add the sage and thyme.
3. Slowly stir in milk, about a half a cup at a time, and incorporate it well. When the mixture thickens, add more milk. Do not let it boil vigorously, or it will burn. Add chicken bullion and let cook for five minutes. Again, if it thickens too much, add more milk. Adjust taste with more salt and pepper if needed.
4. Just before serving, add the parsley, and about a 1/4 cup more milk; the gravy will thicken quickly as it cools.

NEW YEAR'S DAY BLACK-EYED PEAS

Servings: 16 | Prep: 15m | Cooks: 3h | Total: 3h15m

NUTRITION FACTS

Calories: 120 | Carbohydrates: 16.8g | Fat: 3.4g | Protein: 5.7g | Cholesterol: 9mg

INGREDIENTS

- 1 pound dry black-eyed peas
- 1 pinch garlic powder
- 2 cups chopped cooked ham
- 2 onions, diced
- salt and pepper to taste
- 1 (14.5 ounce) can whole tomatoes

DIRECTIONS

1. Place black-eyed peas in 8 quart pot. Add enough water to fill pot 3/4 full. Stir in ham and diced onions, and season with salt, pepper, and garlic powder. Place tomatoes in a blender or food processor, and blend until the tomatoes are liquefied. Add tomatoes to pot. Bring all ingredients to boil. Cover the pot, and simmer on low heat for 2 1/2 to 3 hours, or until the peas are tender.

FRIED GREEN TOMATOES

Servings: 6 | Prep: 10m | Cooks: 10m | Total: 20m

NUTRITION FACTS

Calories: 310 | Carbohydrates: 29.8g | Fat: 18.7g | Protein: 6.8g | Cholesterol: 103mg

INGREDIENTS

- 1 cup all-purpose flour
- 1 cup crushed saltine crackers
- 1 teaspoon salt
- 2 eggs, beaten
- 1 teaspoon pepper
- 1/2 cup butter
- 5 green tomatoes, sliced 1/2 inch thick

DIRECTIONS

1. In a small bowl, stir together the flour, salt and pepper. Place the crushed saltine crackers in another bowl, and the beaten eggs in a third bowl.
2. Melt the butter in a large skillet over medium heat. Dip each tomato slice in the egg to coat, then in the flour mixture. Dip the floured tomato slice back into the egg, and then into the cracker crumbs. Place the coated tomato slices in the hot skillet, and fry until golden brown on each side, about 3 to 5 minutes per side. Add more butter to the pan, if necessary. Serve hot.

FLORIDA STRAWBERRY MUFFINS

Servings: 12 | Prep: 10m | Cooks: 20m | Total: 30m

NUTRITION FACTS

Calories: 168 | Carbohydrates: 28g | Fat: 4.9g | Protein: 3.1g | Cholesterol: 41mg

INGREDIENTS

- 1 1/2 cups chopped fresh strawberries
- 1 teaspoon vanilla extract
- 1/2 cup white sugar
- 1 3/4 cups all-purpose flour
- 1/4 cup white sugar
- 1/2 teaspoon baking soda
- 1/4 cup butter, softened
- 1/4 teaspoon salt
- 2 eggs

- 1/4 teaspoon ground nutmeg

DIRECTIONS

1. In a small bowl, combine the strawberries and 1/2 cup sugar. Set aside for 1 hour. Drain, reserving liquid and berries separately.
2. Preheat the oven to 425 degrees F (220 degrees C). Grease a 12 cup muffin tin, or line with paper liners.
3. In a medium bowl, cream together the butter and 1/4 cup sugar until light and fluffy. Beat in the eggs one at a time, then stir in the vanilla. Combine the flour, baking soda, salt and nutmeg; stir into the creamed mixture alternately with the juice from the berries. Gently stir in the berries. Spoon batter into the prepared muffin cups.
4. Bake for 18 to 20 minutes in the preheated oven, or until the tops spring back when lightly touched. Cool in the pan on a wire rack.

SOUTHERN FRIED CABBAGE WITH BACON, MUSHROOMS, AND ONIONS

Servings: 10 | Prep: 15m | Cooks: 30m | Total: 45m

NUTRITION FACTS

Calories: 123 | Carbohydrates: 9.6g | Fat: 6.4g | Protein: 8g | Cholesterol: 16mg

INGREDIENTS

- 1 pound bacon
- 1 (8 ounce) package sliced fresh mushrooms
- 1 large head cabbage, chopped
- salt and ground black pepper to taste
- 1 large onion, chopped

DIRECTIONS

1. Place bacon in a large skillet and cook over medium-high heat, turning occasionally, until evenly browned, about 10 minutes. Drain the bacon slices on paper towels; crumble when cooled. Drain all but 3 tablespoons of bacon drippings from skillet.
2. Cook and stir cabbage, onion, and mushrooms in the remaining bacon drippings until tender and lightly browned, about 20 minutes. Fold bacon into cabbage mixture. Season with salt and black pepper.

LOUISIANA CRAWFISH ETOUFFEE

Servings: 6 | Prep: 15m | Cooks: 15m | Total: 30m

NUTRITION FACTS

INGREDIENTS

- 3 cups long grain white rice
- 1 pound crawfish tails
- 6 cups water
- 2 tablespoons canned tomato sauce
- 3/4 cup butter
- 1 cup water, or as needed
- 1 large onion, chopped
- 6 green onions, chopped
- 1 clove garlic, chopped
- salt and pepper to taste
- 1/4 cup all-purpose flour
- 1 1/2 tablespoons Cajun seasoning, or to taste

DIRECTIONS

1. Combine the rice and 6 cups water in a saucepan, and bring to a boil. Cover, and reduce heat to low. Simmer for 15 to 20 minutes, until rice is tender and water has been absorbed.
2. While the rice is cooking, melt the butter in a large skillet over medium heat. Add the onion, and saute until transparent. Stir in the garlic, and cook for a minute. Stir in the flour until well blended. Gradually stir in the tomato sauce and remaining 1 cup water, then add the crawfish tails and bring to a simmer. Add the green onions and season with salt, pepper, and Cajun seasoning. Simmer for 5 to 10 minutes over low heat, until the crawfish is cooked but not tough. Serve over hot cooked rice.

GREEN TOMATO RELISH

Servings: 192 | Prep: 1h15m | Cooks: 45m | Total: 2h

NUTRITION FACTS

Calories: 32 | Carbohydrates: 7.6g | Fat: 0.1g | Protein: 0.5g | Cholesterol: 0mg

INGREDIENTS

- 24 large green tomatoes
- 3 tablespoons mustard seed
- 3 red bell peppers, halved and seeded
- 1 tablespoon salt
- 3 green bell peppers, halved and seeded
- 5 cups white sugar
- 12 large onions
- 2 cups cider vinegar

- 3 tablespoons celery seed

DIRECTIONS

1. In a grinder or food processor, coarsely grind tomatoes, red bell peppers, green bell peppers, and onions. (You may need to do this in batches.) Line a large colander with cheesecloth, place in sink or in a large bowl, and pour in tomato mixture to drain for 1 hour.
2. In a large, non-aluminum stockpot, combine tomato mixture, celery seed, mustard seed, salt, sugar, and vinegar. Bring to a boil and simmer over low heat 5 minutes, stirring frequently.
3. Sterilize enough jars and lids to hold relish (12 one-pint jars, or 6 one-quart jars). Pack relish into sterilized jars, making sure there are no spaces or air pockets. Fill jars all the way to top. Screw on lids.
4. Place a rack in the bottom of a large stockpot and fill halfway with boiling water. Carefully lower jars into pot using a holder. Leave a 2 inch space between jars. Pour in more boiling water if necessary, until tops of jars are covered by 2 inches of water. Bring water to a full boil, then cover and process for 30 minutes.
5. Remove jars from pot and place on cloth-covered or wood surface, several inches apart, until cool. Once cool, press top of each lid with finger, ensuring that seal is tight (lid does not move up or down at all). Relish can be stored for up to a year.

PHOENICIAN'S KEY LIME PIE

Servings: 8 | Prep: 20m | Cooks: 25m | Total: 10h45m | Additional: 10h

NUTRITION FACTS

Calories: 456 | Carbohydrates: 47.3g | Fat: 26.9g | Protein: 8.7g | Cholesterol: 165mg

INGREDIENTS

- 2/3 cup toasted slivered almonds
- 4 egg yolks
- 1 cup graham cracker crumbs
- 1 (14 ounce) can sweetened condensed milk
- 1/4 cup white sugar
- 1/2 cup key lime juice
- 1 pinch salt
- 3/4 cup cold heavy cream
- 1/4 cup butter, melted
- 1/2 teaspoon grated lime zest

DIRECTIONS

1. Preheat an oven to 350 degrees F (175 degrees C)
2. Pulse the almonds in a food processor until finely ground. Combine the almonds with the graham cracker crumbs, sugar, and salt. Pour in the melted butter and mix until evenly moistened. Press into a 9-inch pie plate.

3. Bake the crust in the preheated oven until golden brown, 10 to 13 minutes.
4. While the crust is baking, beat the egg yolks in a bowl with the condensed milk, cream, and lime zest. Whisk in the lime juice a little at a time to thicken the custard. Pour the custard into the pie crust and return to the oven.
5. Bake in the oven for 15 minutes to help the custard begin to set. Cool to room temperature on a wire rack before covering loosely with plastic wrap and refrigerating overnight.

SWEET POTATO PIE

Servings: 8 | Prep: 20m | Cooks: 1h10m | Total: 1h30m

NUTRITION FACTS

Calories: 310 | Carbohydrates: 47.3g | Fat: 11.8g | Protein: 4.6g | Cholesterol: 55mg

INGREDIENTS

- 1 (9 inch) unbaked pie crust
- 1 tablespoon all-purpose flour
- 2 cups cooked and mashed sweet potatoes
- 1/2 teaspoon salt
- 2 tablespoons butter, softened
- 1/2 cup buttermilk
- 2 eggs, beaten
- 1/4 teaspoon baking soda
- 1 cup white sugar
- 1 teaspoon vanilla extract

DIRECTIONS

1. Preheat oven to 350 degrees F (175 degrees C).
2. Mix together mashed sweet potatoes, butter or margarine, and eggs. In a separate bowl, mix together sugar, flour, and salt. Mix in spices if desired. Add to sweet potato mixture and stir well.
3. Mix together buttermilk and baking soda. Add to sweet potato mixture and stir well. Mix in vanilla extract. Pour filling into pastry shell.
4. Bake in preheated oven for 70 minutes, until set in center.

QUICK LEMON DIJON CHICKEN

Servings: 2 | Prep: 10m | Cooks: 15m | Total: 25m

NUTRITION FACTS

Calories: 301 | Carbohydrates: 10.5g | Fat: 3.1g | Protein: 55g | Cholesterol: 137mg

INGREDIENTS

- 2 skinless, boneless chicken breast halves - cut into 2 inch pieces
- 4 tablespoons Dijon mustard
- 1/4 lime, juiced
- freshly ground black pepper
- 1/2 lemon, juiced
- Creole-style seasoning to taste

DIRECTIONS

1. Place chicken in a skillet over medium heat. Pour in lime and lemon juices, and stir in Dijon, black pepper, and Creole-seasoning. Cook, turning chicken occasionally, until the chicken pieces are done, about 15 minutes.

MUSHROOM SOUP WITHOUT CREAM

Servings: 8 | Prep: 15m | Cooks: 45m | Total: 1h

NUTRITION FACTS

Calories: 81 | Carbohydrates: 9.6g | Fat: 3.8g | Protein: 4.6g | Cholesterol: 8mg

INGREDIENTS

- 2 tablespoons butter
- 1 teaspoon fresh thyme leaves
- 1 cup peeled and sliced carrots
- 2 pounds sliced fresh brown or white mushrooms
- 1 cup sliced onions
- 6 cups chicken stock
- 1 cup sliced leeks (optional)
- salt and pepper to taste
- 1/2 cup sliced celery
- 1/2 cup chopped green onion

DIRECTIONS

1. Melt the butter in a stock pot over medium heat. Add carrots, onions, leeks, and celery. Cook and stir until tender, but not browned, about 10 minutes. Stir in thyme and mushrooms, and continue cooking until mushrooms are soft, about 5 minutes.
2. Pour chicken stock into the pot, and season with salt and pepper. Cover, and simmer over low heat for 30 minutes. Ladle into bowls, and serve with green onions sprinkled on the top.

CHICKEN CASSEROLE MISSISSIPPI

Servings: 6 | Prep: 25m | Cooks: 30m | Total: 55m

NUTRITION FACTS

Calories: 842 | Carbohydrates: 48.8g | Fat: 38.8g | Protein: 71.1g | Cholesterol: 244mg

INGREDIENTS

- 3 1/2 pounds skinless, boneless chicken breast halves
- 1 (10.75 ounce) can condensed cream of mushroom soup
- 1 onion, chopped
- 2 cups crushed buttery round crackers
- 1 teaspoon seasoning salt
- 1/2 cup butter, melted
- 1 (8 ounce) package wide egg noodles
- 7 ounces sour cream
- 1 (10.75 ounce) can condensed cream of chicken soup

DIRECTIONS

1. Preheat oven to 350 degrees F (175 degrees C). Lightly grease a casserole dish.
2. Cut the chicken into bite size pieces. Place the chicken and onion into a large nonstick skillet and sprinkle with seasoning salt. Cook over medium heat, stirring occasionally, until chicken juices run clear and onion is transparent, 5 to 10 minutes
3. Prepare the egg noodles according to package directions. Combine the chicken and onion mixture, soups, and noodles in the prepared casserole dish and toss to mix together evenly. Crush the crackers in a medium bowl. Stir in the butter and sour cream. Mix thoroughly and spread over the chicken mixture.
4. Bake in preheated oven until the top is golden brown, about 30 minutes

MAPLE GLAZED RIBS

Servings: 6 | Prep: 15m | Cooks: 1h25m | Total: 3h40m

NUTRITION FACTS

Calories: 485 | Carbohydrates: 30.5g | Fat: 29.5g | Protein: 24.2g | Cholesterol: 117mg

INGREDIENTS

- 3 pounds baby back pork ribs
- 1 tablespoon cider vinegar
- 3/4 cup maple syrup
- 1 tablespoon Worcestershire sauce

- 2 tablespoons packed brown sugar
- 1/2 teaspoon salt
- 2 tablespoons ketchup
- 1/2 teaspoon mustard powder

DIRECTIONS

1. Place ribs in a large pot, and cover with water. Cover, and simmer for 1 hour, or until meat is tender. Drain, and transfer ribs to a shallow dish.
2. In a small saucepan, stir together the maple syrup, brown sugar, ketchup, vinegar, Worcestershire sauce, salt, and mustard powder. Bring to a low boil, and cook for 5 minutes, stirring frequently. Cool slightly, then pour over ribs, and marinate in the refrigerator for 2 hours.
3. Prepare grill for cooking with indirect heat. Remove ribs from marinade. Transfer marinade to a small saucepan, and boil for several minutes.
4. Lightly oil grate. Cook for about 20 minutes, basting with the cooked marinade frequently, until nicely glazed.

REAL N'AWLINS MUFFULETTA
Servings: 8 | Prep: 40m | Cooks: 1d | Total: 1d40m

NUTRITION FACTS

Calories: 987 | Carbohydrates: 63.2g | Fat: 62.8g | Protein: 41.4g | Cholesterol: 97mg

INGREDIENTS

- 1 cup pimento-stuffed green olives, crushed
- 1 teaspoon dried basil
- 1/2 cup drained kalamata olives, crushed
- 3/4 teaspoon ground black pepper
- 2 cloves garlic, minced
- 1/4 cup red wine vinegar
- 1/4 cup roughly chopped pickled cauliflower florets
- 1/2 cup olive oil
- 2 tablespoons drained capers
- 1/4 cup canola oil
- 1 tablespoon chopped celery
- 2 (1 pound) loaves Italian bread
- 1 tablespoon chopped carrot
- 8 ounces thinly sliced Genoa salami
- 1/2 cup pepperoncini, drained
- 8 ounces thinly sliced cooked ham
- 1/4 cup marinated cocktail onions

- 8 ounces sliced mortadella
- 1/2 teaspoon celery seed
- 8 ounces sliced mozzarella cheese
- 1 teaspoon dried oregano
- 8 ounces sliced provolone cheese

DIRECTIONS

1. To Make Olive Salad: In a medium bowl, combine the green olives, kalamata olives, garlic, cauliflower, capers, celery, carrot, pepperoncini, cocktail onions, celery seed, oregano, basil, black pepper, vinegar, olive oil and canola oil. Mix together and transfer mixture into a glass jar (or other nonreactive container). If needed, pour in more oil to cover. Cover jar or container and refrigerate at least overnight.
2. To Make Sandwiches: Cut loaves of bread in half horizontally; hollow out some of the excess bread to make room for filling. Spread each piece of bread with equal amounts olive salad, including oil. Layer 'bottom half' of each loaf with 1/2 of the salami, ham, mortadella, mozzarella and Provolone. Replace 'top half' on each loaf and cut sandwich into quarters.
3. Serve immediately, or wrap tightly and refrigerate for a few hours; this will allow for the flavors to mingle and the olive salad to soak into the bread.

SOUTHERN-STYLE CHOCOLATE GRAVY

Servings: 12 | Prep: 10m | Cooks: 10m | Total: 20m

NUTRITION FACTS

Calories: 90 | Carbohydrates: 17g | Fat: 2g | Protein: 1.9g | Cholesterol: 6mg

INGREDIENTS

- 1/4 cup cocoa
- 2 cups milk
- 3 tablespoons all-purpose flour
- 1 tablespoon butter, softened
- 3/4 cup white sugar
- 2 teaspoons vanilla

DIRECTIONS

1. Whisk the cocoa, flour, and sugar together in a bowl until there are no lumps. Pour the milk into the mixture and whisk until well incorporated. Transfer the mixture to a saucepan and cook over medium heat, stirring frequently, until its consistency is similar to gravy, 7 to 10 minutes. Remove from heat and stir the butter and vanilla into the mixture until the butter is melted. Serve immediately.

SLOW COOKER BARBEQUE CHICKEN

Servings: 4 | Prep: 10m | Cooks: 4h | Total: 4h10m

NUTRITION FACTS

Calories: 364 | Carbohydrates: 59.9g | Fat: 2.8g | Protein: 23.1g | Cholesterol: 61mg

INGREDIENTS

- 4 skinless, boneless chicken breast halves
- 1/4 cup brown sugar
- 1 (18 ounce) bottle barbeque sauce (such as Sweet Baby Ray's)
- 1 teaspoon garlic powder
- 1/4 cup distilled white vinegar
- 1/2 teaspoon red pepper flake

DIRECTIONS

1. Put chicken breast halves in a slow cooker.
2. Whisk barbeque sauce, vinegar, brown sugar, garlic powder, and red pepper flakes together in a bowl until the sugar dissolves; pour over the chicken.
3. Cook on Low for 4 to 6 hours.

AUTHENTIC, NO SHORTCUTS, LOUISIANA RED BEANS AND RICE

Servings: 8 | Prep: 20m | Cooks: 8h | Total: 8h20m

NUTRITION FACTS

Calories: 556 | Carbohydrates: 61.5g | Fat: 22.3g | Protein: 27.2g | Cholesterol: 50mg

INGREDIENTS

- 1 pound dried red beans, soaked overnight
- 8 cloves garlic, chopped
- 10 cups water
- 1 teaspoon ground black pepper
- 1 pound andouille sausage, sliced into rounds
- 1 teaspoon Creole seasoning, or to taste
- 1 large sweet onion, chopped
- 6 fresh basil leaves, chopped
- 1 green bell pepper, chopped
- 1 ham hock

- 1 jalapeno pepper, seeded and chopped (optional)
- 4 cups cooked rice

DIRECTIONS

1. Place the beans and water into a slow cooker. Heat a skillet over medium-high heat. Brown the sausage in the skillet; remove from the skillet with a slotted spoon and transfer to the slow cooker. Reserve drippings. Add onion, green pepper, jalapeno pepper and garlic to the drippings; cook and stir until tender, about 5 minutes. Transfer everything from the skillet to the slow cooker.
2. Season the mixture with pepper and Creole seasoning. Add the fresh basil leaves and ham hock. Cover and cook on low for about 8 hours, or until beans are tender. If the bean mixture seems too watery, take the lid off the slow cooker and set heat to High to cook until they reach a creamy texture

PRALINES

Servings: 20 | Prep: 30m | Cooks: 15m | Total: 45m

NUTRITION FACTS

Calories: 180 | Carbohydrates: 24.5g | Fat: 9.4g | Protein: 1g | Cholesterol: 10mg

INGREDIENTS

- 1 1/2 cups toasted pecans
- 3/4 cup brown sugar
- 1 1/2 cups white sugar
- 1/2 cup milk
- 3/8 cup butter
- 1 teaspoon vanilla extract

DIRECTIONS

1. Line a baking sheet with aluminum foil.
2. In large saucepan over medium heat, combine pecans, sugar, butter, brown sugar, milk and vanilla. Heat to between 234 and 240 degrees F (112 to 116 degrees C), or until a small amount of syrup dropped into cold water forms a soft ball that flattens when removed from the water and placed on a flat surface.
3. Drop by spoonfuls onto prepared baking sheet. Let cool completely.

SOUTHERN FRIED APPLES

Servings: 4 | Prep: 10m | Cooks: 10m | Total: 20m

NUTRITION FACTS

Calories: 369 | Carbohydrates: 44.9g | Fat: 23.1g | Protein: 0.8g | Cholesterol: 61mg

INGREDIENTS

- 1/2 cup butter
- 2 tablespoons ground cinnamon
- 1/2 cup white sugar
- 4 Granny Smith apples - peeled, cored, and slice

DIRECTIONS

1. Melt butter in a large skillet over medium heat; stir sugar and cinnamon into the hot butter. Add apples and cook until apples begin to break down, 5 to 8 minutes.

HEAVENLY HOT DOG SAUCE

Servings: 12 | Prep: 10m | Cooks: 1h30m | Total: 1h40m

NUTRITION FACTS

Calories: 268 | Carbohydrates: 4.2g | Fat: 19.8g | Protein: 17.2g | Cholesterol: 71mg

INGREDIENTS

- 2 1/2 pounds lean ground beef
- 1/2 tablespoon pepper
- 1 cup water
- 1 tablespoon white sugar
- 1/2 cup tomato sauce
- 1 tablespoon chili powder
- 1/3 cup ketchup
- crushed red pepper flakes to taste
- 1/2 tablespoon salt

DIRECTIONS

1. Crumble ground beef into a Dutch oven over medium heat. Stir in water, and mash ground beef thoroughly with a potato masher. Stir in tomato sauce, ketchup, salt, pepper, sugar, and chili powder; bring to a boil. Reduce heat to low; simmer, 60 to 90 minutes, until the sauce reaches a medium consistency that is not too soupy.

CHICKEN FRIED STEAK

Servings: 4 | Prep: 15m | Cooks: 30m | Total: 45m

NUTRITION FACTS

Calories: 617 | Carbohydrates: 44.4g | Fat: 25.9g | Protein: 45.5g | Cholesterol: 134mg

INGREDIENTS

- 1 pound boneless beef top loin
- 1/4 teaspoon garlic powder
- 2 cups shortening
- 1 cup all-purpose flour
- 1 egg, beaten
- 1/4 cup all-purpose flour
- 1 cup buttermilk
- 1 quart milk
- salt and pepper to taste
- salt and pepper to taste
- 1 pound boneless beef top loin

DIRECTIONS

1. Cut top loin crosswise into 4 (4 ounce) cutlets. Using a glancing motion, pound each cutlet thinly with a moistened mallet or the side of a cleaver.
2. In a large, heavy skillet, heat 1/2 inch shortening to 365 degrees F (185 degrees C).
3. While the shortening is heating, prepare cutlets. In a shallow bowl, beat together egg, buttermilk, salt and pepper. In another shallow dish, mix together garlic powder and 1cup flour. Dip cutlets in flour, turning to evenly coat both sides. Dip in egg mixture, coating both sides, then in flour mixture once again.
4. Place cutlets in heated shortening. Cook until golden brown, turning once. Transfer to a plate lined with paper towels. Repeat with remaining cutlets. Drain grease, reserving 1/2 cup.
5. Using the reserved drippings in the pan, prepare gravy over medium heat. Blend in 1/4 cup flour to form a paste. Gradually add milk to desired consistency, stirring constantly. For a thicker gravy add less milk; for a thinner gravy stir in more. Heat through, and season with salt and pepper to taste. Serve over chicken fried steak.

CHEF JOHN'S PEACH COBBLER

Servings: 6 | Prep: 15m | Cooks: 55m | Total: 1h10m

NUTRITION FACTS

Calories: 562 | Carbohydrates: 99.3g | Fat: 16.9g | Protein: 5.3g | Cholesterol: 46mg

INGREDIENTS

- 5 cups fresh peaches - peeled, pitted, and sliced
- 1/2 cup butter, melted
- 1/8 teaspoon Chinese five-spice powder

- 1 cup white sugar
- 1 teaspoon grated lemon zest
- 1 1/2 cups self-rising flour
- 1 cup white sugar
- 1 1/2 cups milk
- 1 cup water

DIRECTIONS

1. Preheat oven to 350 degrees F (175 degrees C).
2. Combine peaches, Chinese five-spice powder, and lemon zest in a bowl.
3. Stir sugar and water together in saucepan pan over medium heat until simmering, 2 to 3 minutes. Stir in peach mixture; cook and stir for 2 minutes. Remove from heat and set aside.
4. Combine sugar and self-rising flour in a large bowl. Pour in milk; whisk to form a smooth batter.
5. Pour melted butter into a Dutch oven. Pour batter over the melted butter.
6. Gently place peaches and syrup on top of batter. As the cobbler bakes, they will sink down into the batter.
7. Bake until syrup is bubbling and crust has risen and is golden brown, about 50 minutes.

APPLE BUTTER PUMPKIN PIE

Servings: 8 | Prep: 30m | Cooks: 1h | Total: 1h30m

NUTRITION FACTS

Calories: 413 | Carbohydrates: 43.5g | Fat: 21.3g | Protein: 7.5g | Cholesterol: 90mg

INGREDIENTS

- 1 cup canned pumpkin puree
- 1 cup evaporated milk
- 1 cup apple butter
- 1 (9 inch) unbaked deep dish pie crust
- 1/4 cup dark brown sugar
- 3 tablespoons butter
- 1/2 teaspoon ground cinnamon
- 1/2 cup all-purpose flour
- 1/2 teaspoon ground nutmeg
- 1/3 cup dark brown sugar
- 1/4 teaspoon salt
- 1/2 cup chopped pecans
- 3 eggs, beaten

DIRECTIONS

1. Preheat oven to 350 degrees F (175 degrees C).
2. In a large bowl, combine pumpkin, apple butter, 1/4 cup brown sugar, cinnamon, nutmeg, and salt. Stir in eggs and evaporated milk. Pour into prepared pie shell.
3. Bake in preheated oven for 50 to 60 minutes, or until a knife inserted 2 inches from the center comes out clean. Sprinkle streusel topping over the pie, and bake for an additional 15 minutes.
4. To make the streusel topping: In a small bowl, combine butter, flour, and 1/3 cup brown sugar. Stir until mixture resembles coarse crumbs. Stir in pecans.

SPICY SHRIMP CREOLE

Servings: 8 | Prep: 15m | Cooks: 45m | Total: 1h

NUTRITION FACTS

Calories: 240 | Carbohydrates: 17.5g | Fat: 7.6g | Protein: 26.3g | Cholesterol: 173mg

INGREDIENTS

- 3 tablespoons vegetable oil
- 1 teaspoon ground black pepper
- 2 cups julienne celery
- 1/2 teaspoon cayenne pepper
- 2 onions, chopped
- 2 (14.5 ounce) cans crushed tomatoes
- 4 cloves crushed garlic
- 1 (15 ounce) can tomato sauce
- 1 teaspoon white sugar
- 1 bay leaf, crushed
- 2 tablespoons all-purpose flour
- 1 tablespoon hot pepper sauce
- 1 teaspoon salt
- 2 pounds medium shrimp - peeled and deveined

DIRECTIONS

1. Heat oil in a Dutch oven on medium heat. Saute celery, onions, and garlic in the Dutch oven until the onions are pearly white and the celery has begun to soften.
2. Mix sugar, flour, salt, pepper and cayenne pepper into the Dutch oven. Add crushed tomatoes and tomato sauce, both pieces of bay leaf, and hot sauce. Bring the mixture to a boil, then turn the heat to low.
3. Let the mixture simmer for 30 minutes, stirring occasionally.
4. Approximately 15 minutes before serving, add shrimp to the pot and stir well. If necessary, raise the temperature to medium-low to ensure the Creole is bubbling but not burning. Scoop out the bay leaf halves before serving. Serve when the shrimp is pink and thoroughly cooked.

CHEDDAR CHEESE STRAWS

Servings: 48 | Prep: 25m | Cooks: 5m | Total: 30m

NUTRITION FACTS

Calories: 67 | Carbohydrates: 4.1g | Fat: 4.8g | Protein: 2g | Cholesterol: 6mg

INGREDIENTS

- 2 cups all-purpose flour
- 1/4 teaspoon cayenne pepper
- 2 cups shredded sharp Cheddar cheese
- 1/2 teaspoon salt
- 3/4 cup margarine
- 1/2 cup water
- 1 teaspoon baking powder

DIRECTIONS

1. Preheat oven to 400 degrees F (205 degrees C). Grease or line a baking sheet with parchment paper.
2. Combine the flour, baking powder, cayenne pepper, salt, grated cheese and butter or margarine in a bowl and mix until well combined. Add water a little bit at a time to make a very stiff dough.
3. On a lightly floured surface, roll pieces of the dough into just slightly thicker than pencil shaped sticks. Cut sticks into 4 to 5 inch lengths. Arrange the pieces on the baking sheet.
4. Bake at 400 degrees F (205 degrees C) for 5 minutes or until browned.

DAVE'S GEORGIA BLACK EYED PEAS

Servings: 16 | Prep: 15m | Cooks: 8h20m | Total: 16h35m | Additional: 8h

NUTRITION FACTS

Calories: 431 | Carbohydrates: 31.3g | Fat: 25.2g | Protein: 20.8g | Cholesterol: 51mg

INGREDIENTS

- 2 pounds dried black-eyed peas
- 1/2 cup butter
- 12 cups water
- 2 large yellow onions, chopped
- 8 cubes chicken bouillon
- 1 pound cooked ham, cut into bite-size pieces
- 1 pound bacon
- salt and black pepper to taste

DIRECTIONS

1. Rinse, pick over, and place the peas in a large bowl. Cover with several inches of cool water; let stand 8 hours to overnight.
2. Pour the water into a large saucepan or soup pot. Add the bouillon cubes and bring to a boil, stirring occasionally to dissolve the bouillon. Stir in the peas, reduce heat, and bring to a simmer.
3. Place the bacon in a large, deep skillet and cook over medium-high heat, turning occasionally, until evenly browned, about 10 minutes. Drain the bacon slices on a paper towel-lined plate. Crumble the bacon and set aside.
4. Melt the butter in the pan with the bacon grease; cook and stir the onions until they begin to turn brown at the edges, about 10 minutes. Stir the onions and cooking fat into the peas; add the crumbled bacon, ham, and salt and pepper to taste. Simmer the peas over low heat for 8 hours, stirring every hour.

A SOUTHERN FRIED CHICKEN

Servings: 6 | Prep: 10m | Cooks: 20m | Total: 30m

NUTRITION FACTS

Calories: 806 | Carbohydrates: 79.3g | Fat: 30.3g | Protein: 50.9g | Cholesterol: 183mg

INGREDIENTS

- 3 cups all-purpose flour
- 4 cups buttermilk
- 1 tablespoon seasoned salt
- 1 cup barbeque sauce
- 1 tablespoon garlic powder
- 2 tablespoons Worcestershire sauce
- 1 tablespoon onion powder
- 1 tablespoon steak sauce
- 1 tablespoon coarse ground black pepper
- 1 (3 pound) whole chicken, cut into pieces
- 2 eggs
- 2 cups oil for frying

DIRECTIONS

1. In a large shallow dish, mix together flour, seasoned salt, garlic powder, onion powder, and black pepper. In a separate bowl, beat eggs, then whisk in buttermilk, barbeque sauce, Worcestershire sauce, and steak sauce.
2. Dredge chicken in milk mixture, then in seasoned flour, alternating in each at least twice. Heat oil in a large, deep-sided skillet to 375 degrees F (190 degrees C).
3. Cook chicken in hot oil until golden brown on both sides, about 10 minutes each side.

GOOD OL' ALABAMA SWEET TEA

Servings: 16 | Prep: 1m | Cooks: 10m | Total: 11m

NUTRITION FACTS

Calories: 97 | Carbohydrates: 25g | Fat: 0g | Protein: 0g | Cholesterol: 0mg

INGREDIENTS

- 2 cups sugar
- 3 family sized teabags of orange pekoe tea
- 1/2 gallon water
- 3 cups cold water, or as needed
- 1 tray ice cubes

DIRECTIONS

1. Pour the sugar into a large pitcher. Bring water to a boil in a large pan. When the water begins to boil, remove from the heat, and place the teabags in. Let steep for 5 to 6 minutes.
2. Remove tea bags, and return tea to the heat. Bring just to a boil, then pour into the pitcher, and stir until the sugar is dissolved. Fill the pitcher half way with ice, and stir until most of it melts. Then fill the pitcher the rest of the way with cold water, and stir until blended.

SOUTHERN-STYLE BUTTERMILK FRIED CHICKEN

Servings: 8 | Prep: 30m | Cooks: 30m | Total: 3h | Additional: 2h

NUTRITION FACTS

Calories: 480 | Carbohydrates: 29.4g | Fat: 26.7g | Protein: 29.2g | Cholesterol: 77mg

INGREDIENTS

- 2 cups buttermilk
- 2 cups all-purpose flour
- 1 tablespoon Dijon mustard
- 1 tablespoon baking powder
- 1 teaspoon salt
- 1 tablespoon garlic powder
- 1 teaspoon ground black pepper
- 1 tablespoon onion powder
- 1 teaspoon cayenne pepper
- 5 cups vegetable oil for frying
- 1 whole chicken, cut into pieces

DIRECTIONS

1. Whisk together buttermilk, mustard, salt and pepper, and cayenne in a bowl, and pour into a resealable plastic bag. Add the chicken pieces, coat with the marinade, squeeze out excess air, and seal the bag. Marinate in the refrigerator for 2 to 8 hours.
2. When you are ready to cook the chicken, combine the flour, baking powder, garlic powder, and onion powder in the other plastic bag. Shake to mix thoroughly. Transfer one marinated chicken piece at a time into the dry ingredient bag, and shake well to ensure complete coverage. After all chicken pieces are coated, repeat the process by dipping them in the buttermilk marinade and shaking in the dry coating again.
3. Heat oil in a large frying pan over medium-high heat, making sure not to burn the oil. When oil is hot, fry chicken in batches until golden brown and juices run clear, turning chicken to brown evenly.

RACHAEL'S SUPERHEATED CAJUN BOILED PEANUTS

Servings: 8 | Prep: 20m | Cooks: 1d | Total: 1d20m

NUTRITION FACTS

Calories: 360 | Carbohydrates: 16.2g | Fat: 29.6g | Protein: 16.1g | Cholesterol: 0mg

INGREDIENTS

- 1 pound raw peanuts, in shells
- 1/2 cup salt
- 1 (3 ounce) package dry crab boil (such as Zatarain's Crab and Shrimp Boil)
- 2 tablespoons Cajun seasoning
- 1/2 cup chopped jalapeno peppers
- 1/2 cup red pepper flakes
- 1 tablespoon garlic powder

DIRECTIONS

1. Place peanuts, crab boil, jalapenos, garlic powder, salt, Cajun seasoning, and red pepper flakes into a slow cooker. Pour in water to cover the peanuts and stir to combine. Cover and cook on Low until peanuts are soft, at least 24 hours. Stir occasionally, and add water as needed to keep peanuts covered. Drain; serve hot or cold.

CHEF JOHN'S RED BEANS AND RICE

Servings: 8 | Prep: 30m | Cooks: 3h15m | Total: 3h45m

NUTRITION FACTS

Calories: 542 | Carbohydrates: 62.9g | Fat: 20.5g | Protein: 25.9g | Cholesterol: 46mg

INGREDIENTS

- 1 pound dry red kidney beans
- 1 smoked ham hock
- 1 tablespoon vegetable oil
- 2 bay leaves
- 12 ounces andouille sausage, diced
- 1 teaspoon freshly ground black pepper
- 1 cup finely diced onion
- 1 teaspoon dried thyme
- 3/4 cup chopped celery
- 1/2 teaspoon cayenne pepper, or to taste
- 3/4 cup poblano peppers
- hot sauce to taste
- 4 cloves garlic, minced
- 4 cups cooked white rice
- 2 quarts chicken broth, or more as needed
- 2 tablespoons chopped green onion, or to tast

DIRECTIONS

1. Place beans in a large container and cover with several inches of cool water; let stand 8 hours to overnight. Drain and rinse.
2. Heat vegetable oil in a large pot over medium heat. Cook and stir sausage in hot oil until oils slightly release from sausage and edges brown, 5 to 7 minutes. Stir onion, celery, and poblano pepper into sausage; cook and stir until vegetables soften and start to turn translucent, 5 to 10 minutes. Stir garlic into sausage mixture; cook and stir until fragrant, about 1 minute.
3. Stir red beans, chicken broth, ham hock, bay leaves, black pepper, thyme, cayenne pepper, and hot sauce into the sausage mixture; bring to a boil, reduce heat to low, and simmer gently, stirring occasionally, for 1 1/2 hours. Add salt and continue simmering until beans are soft, meat is tender, and desired consistency is reached, 1 1/2 to 2 hours more. Season with salt.
4. Spoon rice into bowls, ladle red beans mixture over rice, and top with green onion.

FRIED ZUCCHINI

Servings: 4 | Prep: 20m | Cooks: 20m | Total: 40m

NUTRITION FACTS

Calories: 195 | Carbohydrates: 31.3g | Fat: 6.2g | Protein: 4.4g | Cholesterol: 0mg

INGREDIENTS

- 2 zucchini, quartered and sliced
- 1/2 teaspoon salt

- 1 onion, sliced into rings
- 1/2 teaspoon ground black pepper
- 1/2 cup all-purpose flour
- 1/4 teaspoon garlic powder
- 1/2 cup cornmeal
- 1 cup vegetable oil for frying

DIRECTIONS

1. Place zucchini and onions in a medium bowl and mix together.
2. In a small bowl mix flour, cornmeal, salt, pepper and garlic powder.
3. Pour dry mixture over zucchini/onion mixture, cover bowl and shake well. Let mixture sit for about 30 minutes; a batter will form on the vegetables.
4. In a medium skillet heat oil over medium heat. When oil is hot add breaded vegetables and fry, turning to brown evenly.

ZUCCHINI CORN FRITTERS

Servings: 24 | Prep: 15m | Cooks: 4m | Total: 19m

NUTRITION FACTS

Calories: 144 | Carbohydrates: 15g | Fat: 0g | Protein: 3.6g | Cholesterol: 26mg

INGREDIENTS

- 2 cups all-purpose flour
- 1 cup milk
- 1 tablespoon baking powder
- 1/4 cup butter, melted
- 1/2 teaspoon cumin
- 2 cups grated zucchini
- 1/2 cup sugar
- 1 1/2 cups fresh corn, kernels cut from cob
- 1/2 teaspoon salt
- 1 cup finely shredded Cheddar cheese
- fresh ground black pepper
- oil for frying
- 2 eggs, beaten
- 1 cup milk

DIRECTIONS

1. In a large bowl, stir together flour, baking powder, cumin, sugar, salt, and pepper.

2. In a small bowl, whisk together eggs, milk, and butter. Whisk wet ingredients into dry ingredients. Stir in zucchini, corn, and cheese; mix well.
3. Warm oil in a cast iron skillet over medium-high heat. Drop batter by the tablespoonful into hot oil. Fry until crisp and brown, turning once with tongs. Remove to paper towels.

JENNY'S JAMBALAYA

Servings: 6 | Prep: 26m | Cooks: 25m | Total: 50m

NUTRITION FACTS

Calories: 524 | Carbohydrates: 52.4g | Fat: 14.6g | Protein: 44.9g | Cholesterol: 206mg

INGREDIENTS

- 1 tablespoon olive oil
- 1 tablespoon hot sauce
- 2 large onions, chopped
- salt and pepper to taste
- 2 (14.5 ounce) cans stewed tomatoes, drained
- 1 ½ cups uncooked long-grain rice
- 2 boneless chicken breast halves, cooked and shredded
- 3 cups chicken broth
- 1 pound turkey sausage links, without casings, cooked and chopped
- 1 pound large shrimp, peeled and deveined
- ¼ teaspoon garlic powder

DIRECTIONS

1. Select a medium-high setting for an electric skillet; heat oil in hot skillet. Cook onion in oil until soft. Stir in tomatoes, chicken, and sausage. Season with garlic powder, hot sauce, salt, and pepper. Stir in rice, pour in broth, and add shrimp
2. Cover electric skillet. Cook at 300 degrees F (150 degrees C) for about 20 to 25 minutes, or until rice is tender.

GREG'S SOUTHERN BISCUITS

Servings: 8 | Prep: 20m | Cooks: 15m | Total: 35m

NUTRITION FACTS

Calories: 189 | Carbohydrates: 25.6g | Fat: 7.5g | Protein: 4.3g | Cholesterol: 13mg

INGREDIENTS

- 1/2 teaspoon lard

- 2 tablespoons butter, frozen
- 2 cups all-purpose flour
- 2 tablespoons lard, frozen
- 3/4 teaspoon salt
- 1 teaspoon bacon drippings
- 1/4 teaspoon baking soda
- 1 cup buttermilk
- 2 teaspoons baking powder

DIRECTIONS

1. Preheat oven to 450 degrees F (230 degrees C). Lightly grease a baking sheet with 1/2 teaspoon of lard.
2. Mix together the flour, salt, baking soda, and baking powder in a bowl. Grate the frozen butter and 2 tablespoons frozen lard into the flour mixture with a cheese grater; stir lightly 1 or 2 times to mix. With your fingers, make a well in the middle of the flour mixture, and pour the bacon drippings and buttermilk into the well. With just the tips of your fingers, stir lightly and quickly to just bring the dough together before the butter and lard melt. Dough will be sticky.
3. Scrape dough out onto a floured surface, and gently pat the dough flat. Sprinkle the top of the dough with flour, and fold it in half; pat down, fold again, and repeat until you have folded the dough 4 or 5 times. With a rolling pin, roll the dough out to a square about 1 inch thick. Cut the biscuit dough into rounds with a 2 1/2-inch biscuit cutter or the floured edge of a drinking glass by pushing straight down (twisting the cutter will seal the edge and keep the biscuits from rising). Lay the biscuits onto the prepared baking sheet so the edges just touch.
4. Bake in the preheated oven until risen and lightly golden brown, 15 to 20 minutes.

ACCIDENTAL FISH

Servings: 2 | Prep: 10m | Cooks: 20m | Total: 30m

NUTRITION FACTS

Calories: 556 | Carbohydrates: 3g | Fat: 51.7g | Protein: 21.7g | Cholesterol: 204mg

INGREDIENTS

- 2 (4 ounce) fillets mahi mahi
- 1 tablespoon lemon juice
- 2 teaspoons olive oil
- 2 drops Louisiana-style hot sauce, or to taste
- 1/2 cup salted butter
- 1 roma tomato, seeded and chopped (optional)
- 1 clove garlic, minced
- 1 green onion, chopped

DIRECTIONS

1. Preheat an oven to 450 degrees F (230 degrees C).
2. Rub the mahi mahi fillets with the olive oil and lay into a baking dish.
3. Bake in the preheated oven until the fish flakes easily with a fork, about 20 minutes.
4. While the mahi mahi bakes, melt the butter in a saucepan over medium heat.
5. Stir the garlic, lemon juice, and hot sauce into the melted butter; simmer together for 1 minute. Add the tomato and green onion to the butter mixture; cook and stir until hot. Spoon over the baked fish to serve.

BEST BOURBON CHICKEN

Servings: 8 | Prep: 15m | Cooks: 45m | Total: 1h

NUTRITION FACTS

Calories: 417 | Carbohydrates: 36.7g | Fat: 10.9g | Protein: 37.1g | Cholesterol: 97mg

INGREDIENTS

- 4 tablespoons olive oil
- 2 tablespoons apple cider vinegar
- 3 pounds skinless, boneless chicken breast halves - cut into 1 inch pieces
- 2 cloves garlic, minced
- 1 cup water
- 1 tablespoon dried minced onion
- 1 cup packed light brown sugar
- 3/4 teaspoon crushed red pepper flakes, or to taste
- 3/4 cup apple-grape-cherry juice
- 1/2 teaspoon ground ginger
- 2/3 cup soy sauce
- 1/4 cup apple-grape-cherry juice
- 1/4 cup ketchup
- 2 tablespoons cornstarch
- 1/4 cup peach-flavored bourbon liqueur (such as Southern Comfort)

DIRECTIONS

1. Heat the oil in a large heavy pan or Dutch oven, and brown the chicken pieces until lightly golden on all sides, about 10 minutes. Transfer the chicken to a bowl.
2. In the same dutch oven, whisk the water, brown sugar, 3/4 cup of fruit juice cocktail, soy sauce, ketchup, bourbon liqueur, apple cider vinegar, garlic, dried onion, red pepper flakes, and ground ginger into the Dutch oven. Bring the sauce to a boil while scraping the browned bits of food off of the bottom of the pan with a wooden spoon.
3. Stir the chicken back into the sauce, and bring to a full boil over medium-high heat. Reduce the heat to medium-low, and simmer until the sauce is reduced and thickened and the chicken pieces are no longer pink in the middle, about 20 minutes.

4. Remove the chicken pieces to a bowl with a slotted spoon. Stir together 1/4 cup of fruit juice cocktail with the cornstarch until smooth, and whisk the cornstarch mixture into the sauce, stirring constantly to avoid lumps. Bring the sauce back to a simmer, let thicken for about 1 minute, and return the chicken pieces to the sauce. Stir to combine, and serve.

SOUTHERN FRIED CHICKEN LIVERS
Servings: 4 | Prep: 10m | Cooks: 10m | Total: 20m

NUTRITION FACTS

Calories: 470 | Carbohydrates: 27.5g | Fat: 28.9g | Protein: 24g | Cholesterol: 459mg

INGREDIENTS

- 1 pound chicken livers
- 1 tablespoon garlic powder
- 1 egg
- salt and pepper to taste
- 1/2 cup milk
- 1 quart vegetable oil for frying
- 1 cup all-purpose flour

DIRECTIONS

1. Place the chicken livers in a colander, and rinse with water. Drain the livers well. Whisk together the egg and milk in a shallow bowl until well blended. Place the flour, garlic powder, and salt and pepper in a resealable plastic zipper bag, and shake to combine.
2. Heat oil in a deep-fryer or large saucepan to 375 degrees F (190 degrees C).
3. Place the chicken livers in the bowl of egg and milk mixture, and coat each liver. Place the livers, one at a time, into the plastic bag of flour mixture, and shake the bag to coat the each liver completely.
4. Gently place the coated livers, a few at a time, into the hot oil. Cover the pan of oil with a frying screen to avoid getting burned by spatters of oil that will pop out as the livers fry. Deep fry the livers until crisp and golden brown, 5 to 6 minutes.

TEXAS COWBOY BAKED BEANS
Servings: 12 | Prep: 15m | Cooks: 2h | Total: 2h15m

NUTRITION FACTS

Calories: 360 | Carbohydrates: 50g | Fat: 12.4g | Protein: 14.6g | Cholesterol: 43mg

INGREDIENTS

- 1 pound ground beef
- 1/2 cup brown sugar
- 4 (16 ounce) cans baked beans with pork
- 1 tablespoon garlic powder
- 1 (4 ounce) can canned chopped green chile peppers
- 1 tablespoon chili powder
- 1 small Vidalia onion, peeled and chopped
- 3 tablespoons hot pepper sauce (e.g. Tabasco), or to taste
- 1 cup barbeque sauce

DIRECTIONS

1. In a skillet over medium heat, brown the ground beef until no longer pink; drain fat, and set aside.
2. In a 3 1/2 quart or larger slow cooker, combine the ground beef, baked beans, green chiles, onion and barbeque sauce. Season with brown sugar, garlic powder, chili powder and hot pepper sauce. Cook on HIGH for 2 hours, or low for 4 to 5 hours.

OKLAHOMA BRISKET

Servings: 8 | Prep: 30m | Cooks: 4h | Total: 4h30m

NUTRITION FACTS

Calories: 615 | Carbohydrates: 35.6g | Fat: 39.2g | Protein: 30g | Cholesterol: 117mg

INGREDIENTS

- 1/2 cup honey
- 3/4 cup ketchup
- 3 tablespoons soy sauce
- 1/4 cup packed brown sugar
- seasoned salt to taste
- 2 tablespoons Worcestershire sauce
- 1 (5 pound) beef brisket
- 1/4 cup apple cider vinegar
- 1 cup apple cider
- seasoned salt to taste
- seasoned salt to taste
- 1/2 teaspoon garlic powder, or to taste

DIRECTIONS

1. Preheat the oven to 300 degrees F (150 degrees C). Season the brisket all over with seasoned salt, and place in a roasting pan. Pour the apple juice over it, and cover tightly with aluminum foil.
2. Roast the brisket for 3 hours in the preheated oven. Don't peek.

3. Prepare a grill for low heat. In a small bowl, stir together the honey and soy sauce, and season with seasoned salt.
4. When the roast comes out of the oven, place it on the preheated grill. Grill for 30 minutes, turning frequently and basting with the honey sauce.
5. Meanwhile, in a saucepan over low heat, make a barbeque sauce by combining the ketchup, brown sugar, Worcestershire sauce, cider vinegar, seasoned salt, and garlic powder. Cook and stir over low heat for 15 minutes without allowing the sauce to boil. If you boil the sauce, it becomes very vinegary.
6. Let the brisket rest for about 10 minutes after it comes off the grill. Slice and serve with the barbeque sauce.

SAUSAGE BISCUITS AND GRAVY

Servings: 4 | Prep: 10m | Cooks: 20m | Total: 30m

NUTRITION FACTS

Calories: 947 | Carbohydrates: 66.1g | Fat: 59.8g | Protein: 38.4g | Cholesterol: 128mg

INGREDIENTS

- 1 (19 ounce) can Southern-style flaky refrigerated biscuits (such as Pillsbury Grands)
- 11/2 cups milk
- 1 (16 ounce) package maple-flavored breakfast sausage
- 1/2 teaspoon salt
- 3 tablespoons all-purpose flour, or as needed
- 1/4 teaspoon ground black pepper
- 1 (12 ounce) can evaporated milk
- 1 teaspoon butter

DIRECTIONS

1. Preheat oven to 350 degrees F (175 degrees C).
2. Arrange biscuits about 1 1/2 inches apart on a baking sheet.
3. Bake in the preheated oven until golden brown, 13 to 17 minutes. Slice cooked biscuits in half crosswise and keep warm.
4. While biscuits are baking, crumble sausage into a large skillet over medium heat; cook, breaking meat apart, until no longer pink inside, about 10 minutes. Sprinkle sausage and pan drippings with flour and cook and stir until sausage is coated, about 1 more minute. Reduce heat to medium-low.
5. Pour evaporated milk into sausage mixture, followed by milk; stir until thoroughly combined. Bring to a simmer, stirring constantly, and cook until gravy is your desired thickness, 3 to 5 minutes. Season with salt and ground black pepper. Stir butter into gravy until melted. Stir in more flour if gravy isn't thick enough.
6. lace biscuits with cut sides up on serving plates; top with sausage gravy.

KEY WEST PENNE

Servings: 6 | Prep: 5m | Cooks: 15m | Total: 20m

NUTRITION FACTS

Calories: 911 | Carbohydrates: 75.8g | Fat: 48.3g | Protein: 49g | Cholesterol: 260mg

INGREDIENTS

- 1 (16 ounce) package penne pasta
- 1 (8 ounce) jar sun-dried tomatoes, packed in oil
- 1 pound shrimp
- 1 pint heavy cream
- 1 pound scallops
- 1 cup grated Parmesan cheese
- 1 (12 ounce) jar marinated artichoke hearts, drained
- 1/2 cup pitted kalamata olives

DIRECTIONS

1. Bring a large pot of lightly salted water to a boil. Add pasta and cook for 8 to 10 minutes or until al dente; drain.
2. Heat a large heavy skillet over medium heat. Combine shrimp, scallops, artichokes and sun dried tomatoes, then cook until shrimp turn pink. Reduce heat, and stir in cream and parmesan. Toss with cooked pasta, and sprinkle olives on top.

CHARLESTON SHRIMP 'N' GRAVY

Servings: 4 | Prep: 20m | Cooks: 20m | Total: 40m

NUTRITION FACTS

Calories: 263 | Carbohydrates: 12.6g | Fat: 11.1g | Protein: 27.5g | Cholesterol: 196mg

INGREDIENTS

- 3 slices bacon
- 2 tablespoons butter
- 1 onion, chopped
- 4 tablespoons all-purpose flour, divided
- 1 green bell pepper, seeded and chopped
- 1 pound large shrimp, peeled and deveined
- 2 teaspoons seasoned salt with no MSG
- 1 1/2 cups chicken stock
- ground black pepper to taste

- 1 green onion, chopped
- garlic powder to taste

DIRECTIONS

1. Place the bacon in a large skillet over medium heat. Fry until browned, then remove to paper towels to drain. Add the butter to the bacon grease. When the butter begins to sizzle, sprinkle 3 tablespoons of flour over it. Reduce the heat to medium-low, and cook for about 12 minutes, stirring frequently, until dark brown. Don't let it scorch - if it starts to, just reduce the heat.

2. When the roux reaches dark brown, increase the heat to medium-high, and add the onions and bell pepper. Cook and stir for a couple of minutes, just until softened. Meanwhile, place the shrimp in a bowl, and toss with seasoned salt, pepper, garlic powder, and remaining flour. Pour into the pan, and stir constantly for 1 minute. Whisk in the chicken stock, and reduce the heat to low. Cook for just a few minutes to thicken the broth. Don't cook much longer, or the shrimp will become tough. Sprinkle the chopped green onion over it, and remove from the heat. Serve over fresh hot grits, rice or biscuits. Crumble the bacon slices on top.

GRANNY'S BANANA BREAD

Servings: 12 | Prep: 15m | Cooks: 1h | Total: 1h15m

NUTRITION FACTS

Calories: 298 | Carbohydrates: 53.8g | Fat: 7.7g | Protein: 5.6g | Cholesterol: 35mg

INGREDIENTS

- 2 1/4 cups all-purpose flour
- 1/3 cup unsweetened applesauce
- 1 teaspoon baking soda
- 4 ripe bananas, mashed
- 1/2 teaspoon ground cinnamon
- 1 tablespoon vanilla extract
- 1/2 teaspoon ground nutmeg
- 1 cup raisins (optional)
- 1 cup white sugar
- 1 cup chopped walnuts (optional)
- 2 eggs
- 1/3 cup unsweetened applesauce

DIRECTIONS

1. Preheat oven to 375 degrees F (190 degrees C). Lightly grease and flour a 9x5 inch loaf pan.

2. In a large bowl, stir together flour, baking soda, cinnamon, nutmeg and white sugar. Stir in eggs, applesauce, bananas and vanilla extract. Fold in raisins and nuts if desired. Pour batter into prepared pan.
3. Bake in preheated oven for 45 to 60 minutes, until a knife inserted into center of the loaf comes out clean.

BARBEQUED PORK RIBS

Servings: 10 | Prep: 20m | Cooks: 1h20m | Total: 3h40m | Additional: 2h

NUTRITION FACTS

Calories: 544 | Carbohydrates: 17.6g | Fat: 39.5g | Protein: 29.6g | Cholesterol: 144mg

INGREDIENTS

- 5 pounds pork spareribs, cut into serving size pieces
- 1 cup water
- 1/2 cup butter
- 1 cup ketchup
- 1 medium onion, chopped
- 1 cup hickory smoke flavored barbeque sauce
- 1 tablespoon minced garlic
- 1 lemon, juiced
- 1/2 cup distilled white vinegar
- salt and pepper to taste

DIRECTIONS

1. Place ribs in large skillet or roasting pan. Cover with lightly salted water, and bring to a boil. Reduce heat to low, and simmer for 1 hour, or until meat is tender, but not quite falling off the bone. Remove from heat, and drain.
2. Place the boiled ribs in a roasting pan, and cover with sauce. Cover, and refrigerate for at least 2 hours.
3. Melt butter in a saucepan over medium heat. Cook the onion and garlic in butter until the onion is tender; remove from heat. In a blender, combine 1 cup water, vinegar, ketchup, barbeque sauce, and lemon juice. Pour in the melted butter mixture, and puree for 1 minute. Pour into a saucepan, and season to taste with salt and pepper. Bring to a boil, then remove from heat.
4. Preheat grill for medium-high heat.
5. Brush grill grate with oil. Grill ribs for 10 to 20 minutes, or until well browned, basting with sauce and turning frequently.

GINGERBREAD COOKIES

Servings: 60 | Prep: 30m | Cooks: 12m | Total: 1h | Additional: 18m

NUTRITION FACTS

INGREDIENTS

- 1 cup white sugar
- 1 cup margarine, melted
- 2 teaspoons ground ginger
- 1/2 cup evaporated milk
- 1 teaspoon ground nutmeg
- 1 cup unsulfured molasses
- 1 teaspoon ground cinnamon
- 3/4 teaspoon vanilla extract
- 1/2 teaspoon salt
- 3/4 teaspoon lemon extract
- 1 1/2 teaspoons baking soda
- 4 cups unbleached all-purpose flour

DIRECTIONS

1. Preheat oven to 375 degrees F (190 degrees C). Lightly grease cookie sheets.
2. In a large bowl, stir together the sugar, ginger, nutmeg, cinnamon, salt, and baking soda. Mix in the melted margarine, evaporated milk, molasses, vanilla, and lemon extracts. Stir in the flour, 1 cup at a time, mixing well after each addition. The dough should be stiff enough to handle without sticking to fingers. If necessary, increase flour by up to 1/2 cup to prevent sticking
3. When the dough is smooth, roll it out to 1/4 inch thick on a floured surface, and cut into cookies. Place cookies on the prepared cookie sheets.
4. Bake for 10 to 12 minutes in the preheated oven. The cookies are done when the top springs back when touched. Remove from cookie sheets to cool on wire racks.

CAJUN CORN AND CRAB BISQUE

Servings: 8 | Prep: 20m | Cooks: 30m | Total: 50m

NUTRITION FACTS

Calories: 387 | Carbohydrates: 16.3g | Fat: 30.1g | Protein: 14.8g | Cholesterol: 131mg

INGREDIENTS

- 3 tablespoons butter
- 1 bay leaf
- 3 tablespoons all-purpose flour
- 2 cups milk
- 1 tablespoon vegetable oil
- 2 cups heavy cream

* 1 large onion, chopped
* 1 teaspoon liquid shrimp and crab boil seasoning
* 1 tablespoon minced garlic
* 1 pound fresh lump crabmeat
* 1 large celery stalk, minced
* 1/4 cup chopped green onions
* Cajun seasoning to taste
* 1/2 teaspoon Worcestershire sauce
* 1 cup chicken broth
* salt and black pepper to taste
* 1 1/2 cups frozen corn kernels
* Additional chopped green onions

DIRECTIONS

1. Melt the butter in a small saucepan over medium heat; then gradually whisk in the flour. Cook 5 to 7 minutes, whisking constantly, until a golden roux forms; set aside.
2. Heat the oil in a Dutch oven over medium heat. Combine the onion, garlic, and celery and cook 1 minute. Add the Cajun seasoning to taste. Stir in the broth, corn, and bay leaf. Bring to a simmer, then pour in the milk, cream, and liquid crab boil. When the mixture begins to simmer, reduce heat to low and simmer 7 minutes. Stir in the roux, 1 tablespoon at a time, blending thoroughly. Continue to cook, on low heat, whisking until mixture thickens. Stir in crabmeat, green onions, and Worcestershire sauce. Simmer 6 to 8 minutes more. Season with salt and pepper to taste.

CREOLE CHICKEN

Servings: 8 | Prep: 15m | Cooks: 5h20m | Total: 5h35m

NUTRITION FACTS

Calories: 389 | Carbohydrates: 27.9g | Fat: 19.2g | Protein: 24.5g | Cholesterol: 81mg

INGREDIENTS

* 8 chicken thighs
* 1 teaspoon salt
* 1/4 pound cooked ham, cut into one inch cubes
* 2 dashes hot pepper sauce
* 1 (16 ounce) can diced tomatoes
* 2 cups water
* 1 green bell pepper, chopped
* 1 cup uncooked long grain white rice
* 6 green onions, chopped
* 1/2 pound Polish sausage, sliced diagonally
* 1 (6 ounce) can tomato paste

DIRECTIONS

1. In a slow cooker, place the chicken, ham, tomatoes, bell pepper, green onions, tomato paste, salt, and hot pepper sauce. Cover, and cook on Low for 4 to 5 hours.
2. Combine water and rice in a medium saucepan. Bring to a boil. Reduce heat, cover, and simmer for 20 minute
3. Mix the cooked rice and sausage into the slow cooker. Cover, and cook on High for 15 to 20 minutes, or until the sausage is heated through.

KENTUCKY BANANA PUDDING

Servings: 8 | Prep: 20m | Cooks: 20m | Total: 1h40

NUTRITION FACTS

Calories: 461 | Carbohydrates: 79.1g | Fat: 13.4g | Protein: 8g | Cholesterol: 41mg

INGREDIENTS

- 1 cup white sugar
- 1 1/2 cups milk
- 1/4 cup cornstarch
- 2 teaspoons vanilla extract
- 1 egg, beaten
- 1 (12 ounce) package vanilla wafers
- 1 (12 fluid ounce) can evaporated milk
- 4 banana, sliced

DIRECTIONS

1. In a saucepan over medium heat, combine the sugar, cornstarch, egg, evaporated milk and regular milk. Mix together well and stir until thick. Remove from heat; add vanilla and mix well.
2. In a large bowl or casserole dish, arrange a layer of cookies. Pour pudding mixture over cookies and top with a layer of sliced bananas. Refrigerate until chilled.

CINNAMON-SUGAR POPCORN

Servings: 16 | Prep: 5m | Cooks: 40m | Total: 1h45m

NUTRITION FACTS

Calories: 114 | Carbohydrates: 17.8g | Fat: 4.4g | Protein: 1.6g | Cholesterol: 10mg

INGREDIENTS

- 1 cup unpopped popcorn
- 2 teaspoons ground cinnamon

- 1/3 cup butter
- 1/2 teaspoon salt
- 2/3 cup white sugar
- 1/2 teaspoon vanilla extract

DIRECTIONS

1. Preheat an oven to 250 degrees F (120 degrees C). Pop the popcorn using an air popper according to manufacturer's directions. Place into a large mixing bowl, and set aside.
2. Melt the butter in a small saucepan over medium heat. Stir in the sugar, cinnamon, salt, and vanilla, and cook until thick and bubbly. Pour over the popcorn, and stir until the popcorn is evenly coated. Spread the popcorn into a large roasting pan.
3. Bake in the preheated oven 10 minutes, then turn the heat off, and allow the popcorn to stay in the oven 20 minutes longer. Remove from oven, and cool completely before serving.

FRANK'S SPICY ALABAMA ONION BEER CHILI

Servings: 8 | Prep: 20m | Cooks: 2h | Total: 2d2h20m

NUTRITION FACTS

Calories: 369 | Carbohydrates: 40g | Fat: 14.2g | Protein: 23.2g | Cholesterol: 52mg

INGREDIENTS

- 2 pounds ground beef chuck
- 1/4 cup Worcestershire sauce
- 2 large white onions, chopped
- 3 tablespoons hot pepper sauce (e.g. Tabasco), or to taste
- 2 (14.5 ounce) cans diced tomatoes with juice
- 1/3 cup chili powder
- 2 (15 ounce) cans tomato sauce
- 4 fresh jalapeno peppers, seeded and chopped
- 1 (12 fluid ounce) can beer
- 3 tablespoons red pepper flakes, or to taste (optional)
- 2 (15 ounce) cans spicy chili beans

DIRECTIONS

1. Crumble the ground chuck into a skillet over medium heat. Cook, stirring occasionally until evenly browned. Drain grease. Transfer the beef to a large soup pot. Add onions, diced tomatoes, tomato sauce, beer and chili beans. Season with Worcestershire sauce, hot pepper sauce, chili powder, jalapenos, and red pepper flakes, if using.
2. Cover the pot, and simmer over low heat for 2 hours. Turn off heat, and let cool, then refrigerate for two days. It gets much better with time. Heat and serve.

CAJUN CAKE

Servings:12 | Prep: 30m | Cooks: 1h | Total: 1h30m

NUTRITION FACTS

Calories: 492 | Carbohydrates: 76.5g | Fat: 19g | Protein: 6.8g | Cholesterol: 36mg

INGREDIENTS

- 3 cups all-purpose flour
- 1 (20 ounce) can crushed pineapple with juice
- 1 1/2 cups white sugar
- 3/4 cup evaporated milk
- 2 teaspoons baking soda
- 1/2 cup margarine
- 1/4 teaspoon salt
- 1 cup chopped pecans
- 2 eggs
- 1 1/2 cups flaked coconut
- 3/4 cup white sugar

DIRECTIONS

1. Preheat oven to 350 degrees F (175 degrees C). Grease and flour a 9x13-inch pan.
2. In a large bowl, sift together flour, 1 1/2 cup sugar, salt and baking soda. Add eggs, pineapple, and juice. Mix at low speed until well blended.
3. Pour batter into prepared pan. Bake in preheated oven until a tester comes out clean, 30 to 35 minutes. Have the topping ready when the cake comes out of the oven.
4. To Make Topping: In a saucepan, combine milk, 3/4 cup sugar, and margarine. Bring to a boil and cook for 2 minutes, stirring constantly. Add pecans and coconut and combine. Remove from heat.
5. When cake comes out of the oven, pour on the topping and carefully spread on while cake is still hot.

KENTUCKY BOURBON BALLS

Servings: 24 | Prep: 20m | Cooks: 10m | Total: 16h30m

NUTRITION FACTS

Calories: 252 | Carbohydrates: 31.3g | Fat: 13.9g | Protein: 2.3g | Cholesterol: 10mg

INGREDIENTS

- 1 cup chopped nuts
- 1 (16 ounce) package confectioners' sugar
- 5 tablespoons Kentucky bourbon

- 18 ounces semisweet chocolate
- 1/2 cup butter, softened

DIRECTIONS

1. Place the nuts in a sealable jar. Pour the bourbon over the nuts. Seal and allow to soak overnight.
2. Mix the butter and sugar; fold in the soaked nuts. Form into 3/4" balls and refrigerate overnight.
3. Line a tray with waxed paper. Melt the chocolate in the top of a double boiler over just-barely simmering water, stirring frequently and scraping down the sides with a rubber spatula to avoid scorching. Roll the balls in the melted chocolate to coat; arrange on the prepared tray. Store in refrigerator until serving.

REAL SOUTHERN CORNBREAD

Servings: 12 | Prep: 10m | Cooks: 50m | Total: 1h

NUTRITION FACTS

Calories: 369 | Carbohydrates: 36.3g | Fat: 22g | Protein: 7.7g | Cholesterol: 34mg

INGREDIENTS

- 2 cups cornmeal
- 2 eggs
- 2 cups all-purpose flour
- 1 cup margarine, melted
- 1/2 teaspoon salt
- 4 cups buttermilk
- 2 tablespoons baking powder
- 1/4 cup corn oil

DIRECTIONS

1. In a large bowl mix together the corn meal, flour, salt, and baking powder.
2. In a separate bowl mix together the eggs, butter, and buttermilk. Add to the dry ingredients and stir until well blended.
3. Heat a dry 12 inch cast iron skillet over high heat for 2 minutes. Add corn oil to skillet, swirl oil around to coat bottom and sides. Leave remaining oil in pan. Return to high heat for 1 minute.
4. Pour the cornbread batter into the skillet and cook on high heat until bubbles start to form in the center. Remove from stove.
5. Bake in a preheated 400 degree F (200 degree C) oven for 40 to 50 minutes, or until a knife inserted into the center comes out clean. Serve warm.

SPINACH SALAD WITH PEACHES AND PECANS

Servings: 4 | Prep: 10m | Cooks: 10m | Total: 20m

NUTRITION FACTS

Calories: 253 | Carbohydrates: 11.4g | Fat: 22.6g | Protein: 2.9g | Cholesterol: 5mg

INGREDIENTS

- 3/4 cup pecans
- 4 cups baby spinach, rinsed and dried
- 2 ripe peaches
- 1/4 cup poppyseed salad dressing

DIRECTIONS

1. Preheat oven to 350 degrees F (175 degrees C). Arrange pecans on a single layer on a baking sheet and roast in preheated oven for 7-10 minutes, until they just begin to darken. Remove from oven and set aside.
2. Peel peaches (if desired) and slice into bite-sized segments. Combine peaches, spinach and pecans in a large bowl. Toss with dressing until evenly coated, adding a little additional dressing, if necessary.

CREAM OF ASPARAGUS AND MUSHROOM SOUP

Servings: 8 | Prep: 15m | Cooks: 40m | Total: 55m

NUTRITION FACTS

Calories: 171 | Carbohydrates: 12.7g | Fat: 11.8g | Protein: 5.2g | Cholesterol: 29mg

INGREDIENTS

- 3 slices bacon
- 6 cups chicken broth
- 1 tablespoon bacon drippings
- 1 potato, peeled and diced
- 1/4 cup butter
- 1 pound fresh asparagus, tips set aside and stalks chopped
- 3 stalks celery, chopped
- salt and ground black pepper to taste
- 1 onion, diced
- 1 (8 ounce) package sliced fresh mushrooms
- 3 tablespoons all-purpose flour
- 3/4 cup half-and-half cream

DIRECTIONS

1. Place the bacon in a large, deep skillet, and cook over medium-high heat, turning occasionally, until evenly browned, about 10 minutes. Drain the bacon slices on a paper towel-lined plate. Crumble bacon when cool; set aside. Reserve 1 tablespoon of bacon drippings.
2. Melt butter with drippings in a saucepan over medium heat.
3. Cook and stir celery and onion in the saucepan until onion is translucent, about 4 minutes.
4. Whisk flour into the mixture and cook for 1 minute.
5. Whisk in chicken broth and bring to a boil.
6. Add potato and chopped asparagus stalks, reserving the asparagus tips for later. Season with salt and ground black pepper.
7. Reduce heat and simmer for 20 minutes.
8. Pour the soup into a blender, filling the pitcher no more than halfway full. Hold down the lid of the blender with a folded kitchen towel, and carefully start the blender, using a few quick pulses to get the soup moving before leaving it on to puree. Puree in batches until smooth and pour into a clean pot. Alternately, you can use a stick blender and puree the soup right in the cooking pot.
9. Cook and stir mushrooms and asparagus tips in the same skillet used for bacon until mushrooms give up their liquid, 5 to 8 minutes. Season with salt and ground black pepper, if needed.
10. Stir mushrooms, asparagus tips, and half-and-half cream to pureed soup. Cook until thoroughly heated.
11. Garnish soup with crumbled bacon.

PEPPERONI ROLL

Servings: 20 | Prep: 25m | Cooks: 15m | Total: 2h10m

NUTRITION FACTS

Calories: 247 | Carbohydrates: 31.6g | Fat: 10.3g | Protein: 6.6g | Cholesterol: 43mg

INGREDIENTS

- 1 cup warm water (100 degrees F/40 degrees C)
- 2 teaspoons salt
- 1/2 teaspoon white sugar
- 2 eggs, beaten
- 1 (.25 ounce) package active dry yeast
- 1/2 cup butter, melted
- 5 cups all-purpose flour
- 2 teaspoons salt
- 3/4 cup white sugar

DIRECTIONS

1. Dissolve 1/2 teaspoon sugar in 1 cup of warm water in a small bowl. Sprinkle yeast over the water and let stand for 5 minutes.
2. Mix flour, 3/4 cup sugar, and salt in a large bowl. Stir in the yeast mixture, beaten eggs, and melted butter. When the dough has pulled together, turn it out onto a lightly floured surface and knead until smooth and elastic, about 8 minutes.

3. Lightly oil a large bowl, then place the dough in the bowl and turn to coat with oil. Cover with a light cloth and let rise in a warm place (80 to 95 degrees F (27 to 35 degrees C)) until doubled in volume, about 1 1/2 hours.
4. Preheat an oven to 350 degrees F (175 degrees C). Grease a cookie sheet.
5. Punch down the dough, and divide it into 20 equal pieces about the size of a golf ball. Using your hands, flatten each piece into a small rectangle about 4 inches square. Place 3 slices of pepperoni down the center of each dough square, overlapping the slices. Place another row of 3 slices next to the first. Roll the dough around the pepperoni slices, pinch the edges closed, and place the rolls on the prepared cookie sheet.
6. Bake the rolls in the preheated oven for 14 to 16 minutes, until the bottoms are lightly browned and the tops are barely golden.

BEST BUCKWHEAT PANCAKES

Servings: 2 | Prep: 5m | Cooks: 10m | Total: 15m

NUTRITION FACTS

Calories: 560 | Carbohydrates: 42.1g | Fat: 39g | Protein: 12.8g | Cholesterol: 189mg

INGREDIENTS

- 1 cup buttermilk
- 1 teaspoon white sugar
- 1 egg
- 1/2 teaspoon salt
- 3 tablespoons butter, melted
- 1 teaspoon baking soda
- 6 tablespoons all-purpose flour
- 3 tablespoons butter
- 6 tablespoons buckwheat flour

DIRECTIONS

1. In a medium bowl, whisk together the buttermilk, egg, and melted butter.
2. In another bowl, mix together white flour, buckwheat flour, sugar, salt and baking soda. Pour the dry ingredients into the egg-mixture. Stir until the two mixtures are just incorporated.
3. Heat a griddle or large frying pan to medium-hot, and place 1 tablespoon of butter, margarine or oil into it. Let the butter melt before spooning the batter into the frying pan, form 4 inch pancakes out of the batter. Once bubbles form on the top of the pancakes, flip them over, and cook them on the other side for about 3 minutes. Continue with this process until all of the batter has been made into pancakes.

MINT TEA PUNCH

Servings: 10 | Prep: 10m | Cooks: 0m | Total: 10m

NUTRITION FACTS

Calories: 94 | Carbohydrates: 24.2g | Fat: 0.1g | Protein: 0.4g | Cholesterol: 0mg

INGREDIENTS

- 3 cups boiling water
- 1/4 cup lemon juice
- 12 sprigs fresh mint
- 5 cups cold water
- 4 tea bags
- 3 orange slices for garnish (optional)
- 1 cup white sugar
- 3 lemon slices for garnish (optional
- 1 cup orange juice

DIRECTIONS

1. Place the tea bags and mint sprigs into a large pitcher. Pour boiling water over them, and allow to steep for about 8 minutes. Remove and discard the tea bags and mint leaves, squeezing out excess liquid. Stir in sugar until dissolved, then stir in the orange juice and lemon juice. Pour in the cold water. Serve over ice cubes, garnished with orange or lemon slices.

TENNESSEE MEATLOAF

Servings: 10 | Prep: 40m | Cooks: 1h | Total: 1h55m | Additional: 15m

NUTRITION FACTS

Calories: 233 | Carbohydrates: 15.9g | Fat: 11.2g | Protein: 17.1g | Cholesterol: 92mg

INGREDIENTS

- 1/2 cup ketchup
- 1/2 teaspoon ground black pepper
- 1/4 cup brown sugar
- 2 teaspoons prepared mustard
- 2 tablespoons cider vinegar
- 2 teaspoons Worcestershire sauce
- cooking spray
- 1/2 teaspoon hot pepper sauce (such as Tabasco)
- 1 onion, chopped
- 1/2 cup milk
- 1/2 green bell pepper, chopped
- 2/3 cup quick cooking oats

- 2 cloves garlic, minced
- 1 pound ground beef
- 2 large eggs, lightly beaten
- 1/2 pound ground pork
- 1 teaspoon dried thyme
- 1/2 pound ground veal
- 1 teaspoon seasoned salt

DIRECTIONS

1. Combine ketchup, brown sugar, and cider vinegar in a bowl; mix well.
2. Preheat oven to 350 degrees F (175 degrees C). Spray two 9x5-inch loaf pans with cooking spray or line with aluminum foil for easier cleanup (see Cook's Note).
3. Place onion and green pepper in covered microwave container and cook until softened, 1 to 2 minutes. Set aside to cool.
4. In large mixing bowl, combine garlic, eggs, thyme, seasoned salt, black pepper, mustard, Worcestershire sauce, hot sauce, milk, and oats. Mix well. Stir in cooked onion and green pepper. Add ground beef, pork, and veal. With gloved hands, work all ingredients together until completely mixed and uniform.
5. Divide meatloaf mixture in half and pat half of mixture into each prepared loaf pan. Brush loaves with half of the glaze; set remainder of glaze aside.
6. Bake in preheated oven for 50 minutes. Remove pans from oven; carefully drain fat. Brush loaves with remaining glaze. Return to oven and bake for 10 minutes more. Remove pans from oven and allow meatloaf to stand for 15 minutes before slicing.

FRESH PEACH COBBLER

Servings: 6 | Prep: 30m | Cooks: 25m | Total: 55m

NUTRITION FACTS

Calories: 243 | Carbohydrates: 42.5g | Fat: 7g | Protein: 2.9g | Cholesterol: 2mg

INGREDIENTS

- 1/2 cup white sugar
- 1 tablespoon white sugar
- 1 tablespoon cornstarch
- 1 1/2 teaspoons baking powder
- 1/4 teaspoon ground cinnamon
- 1/2 teaspoon salt
- 4 cups sliced fresh peaches
- 3 tablespoons shortening
- 1 teaspoon lemon juice
- 1/2 cup milk
- 1 cup all-purpose flour

DIRECTIONS

1. Preheat oven to 400 degrees F (200 degrees C).
2. Combine 1/2 cup sugar, cornstarch, and cinnamon in a saucepan and whisk to mix. Stir in sliced peaches (see Editor's Note) and lemon juice, tossing until peaches are evenly coated.
3. Cook filling over medium heat, stirring constantly, until mixture thickens and boils. Boil 1 minute. Pour mixture into an ungreased 2-quart casserole dish. Keep mixture hot in oven while you make the topping.
4. In a medium bowl combine flour, 1 tablespoon sugar, baking powder, and salt. Mix thoroughly, then cut in shortening until mixture looks like fine crumbs. Add milk and stir until mixture is evenly moistened.
5. Remove peach filling from oven and drop dough onto peaches in 6 equal-size spoonfuls.
6. Return cobbler to oven and bake until topping is golden brown, 25 to 30 minutes.